Beth St

Ditch

Methuen Drama

 HighTide

HighTide
presents

a new play by Beth Steel

First performance as part of HighTide
Festival 2010, The Cut, Halesworth,
Suffolk on 30 April 2010.

London opening at The Old Vic
Tunnels on 13 May 2010.

A co-production with The Old Vic.

CAST

DITCH

a new play by Beth Steel

Sourced, developed and produced
by HighTide

JAMES
GETHIN ANTHONY

TURNER
CRAIG CONWAY

MEGAN
MATTI HOUGHTON

MRS PEEL
DEARBLHA MOLLOY

BUG
PAUL RATTRAY

BURNS
DANNY WEBB

Director: **Richard Twyman**
Producers: **Steven Atkinson,
Samuel Hodges, Nate Sence**
Design: **takis**
Lighting: **Matt Prentice**
Sound: **Christopher Shutt**
Music: **Tom Mills**
Voice: **John Tucker**
Casting: **Camilla Evans & Greer
Dale-Foulkes**
Assistant Director: **Andrea Ferran**
Fight Director: **Bret Yount**
Production Manager: **Jae Forrester**
Stage Manager: **Sarah Jenkins**
Illustration: **Julian Mills**
Press Representation: **David Bloom
at Target Live 020 3372 0950**

HighTide wishes to thank Hamish
Jenkinson, Douglas McJannet, Kevin
Spacey, John Richardson, Kate
Pakenham, Sally Greene, Emily Blacksell,
Catrin John, and Michael Smythe at The
Old Vic; Cathy Bolton and the team at
Waterloo Brasserie; Sebastian Born at the
National Theatre; and Clare Parsons and
Tony Langham at Lansons
Communications for their ongoing
support.

Ditch was first developed through the
Genesis Laboratory, HighTide's Research
and Development Studio at Waterloo
Brasserie supported by the Genesis
Foundation. The cast were: Claire Brown,
Jon Foster, Richard Galazka, John
Hollingworth, Lois Jones and Nikesh
Patel.

CAST

GETHIN ANTHONY (JAMES)
Trained at Oxford University and LAMDA. While at Oxford, Gethin was President of the OUDS.
* For HighTide: *Ditch* (HighTide Festival 2010).
* Other theatre includes: *Cling to Me Like Ivy* (Birmingham Rep); *What Fatima Did* (Hampstead); *Fairytale* (The Old Red Lion); *Death of Cool* (Tristan Bates); *24 Hour Plays* (The Old Vic); *Some Voices* (Old Fire Station); *Cyrano de Bergerac* (Oxford Playhouse); *Twelfth Night* (Oriel Gardens); *Three Sisters* (Oxford Playhouse); *Bash* (Burton Taylor); *Europe* (Oxford Playhouse); *As You Like* It (Oxford Playhouse); *Bald Prima Donna* (Burton Taylor); *Loot!* (Burton Taylor); *Popcorn* (Old Fire Station); *Time at The Bar* (Burton Taylor); *Macbeth* (Bedlam, Edinburgh); and *Comedy of Errors* (Minack Theatre, Cornwall).
* Television includes: *10 Days to War; Doctors; Pinochet's Progress; Holby City.*
* Film includes: *Into The Storm; Beyond the Rave; Bus Terminal.*
* Radio includes: *Legsy Gets a Break* (BBC).

CRAIG CONWAY (TURNER)
* For HighTide: *Ditch* (HighTide Festival 2010).
* Other theatre includes: *Our Friends in the North* (Northern Stage); *Bodies* (Northern Stage); *1984* (Northern Stage); *Animal Farm* (Northern Stage); *Romeo and Juliet* (Northern Stage); *A Clockwork Orange* (Northern Stage); *Macbeth* (Leicester Haymarket); *East* (Leicester Haymarket); *Homage to Catalonia* (West Yorkshire Playhouse); *The Doorman* (Tour); *The Night Shift* (BAC); *Peer Gynt* (National Theatre); and *Romeo and Juliet* (National Theatre).
* Television includes: *Vera; Our Friends in the North; Terry Pratchett's Hogfather; Heatwave; Hollyoaks; Active Defence; and Little Angel.*
* Film includes: *Four; Devil's Playground; Romans 12:20* (Winner New York International Independent Film and Video Festival 2008, Rhode Island International Film Festival 2008 and Arpa International Film Festival 2008); *The Tournament; Doomsday; Vera Drake;* and *Dog Soldiers.*
* Craig has also directed, devised and written a number of projects for the Contact Theatre in Manchester and been Assistant Director on 'To You' for the Lowry Theatre, Manchester.

MATTI HOUGHTON (MEGAN)
Trained at Guildhall School of Music and Drama.
* For HighTide: *I Caught Crabs in Walberswick* (HighTide Festival 2008); *Ditch* (HighTide Festival 2010).
* Other theatre includes: *Caucasian Chalk Circle* (Shared Experience); *Romeo and Juliet* (Exeter Northcott/Ludlow Festival); *Antigone* (Royal Exchange); *The Cracks in My Skin* (Royal Exchange); *Kebab* (Royal Court); *International Residency* (Royal Court); *Kindertransport* (Shared Experience); *Watership Down* (Lyric Hammersmith); *The Menu, Burn, Chatroom and Citizenship* (National Theatre); *Stallerhof* (Southwark Playhouse); and *Mikey the Pikey* (Pleasance Theatre, Edinburgh).
* Television includes: *Law & Order; Pulse; Luther; The Bill; Doctors; Wire in the Blood; Afterlife II; The Last Detective.*

DEARBHLA MOLLOY (MRS PEEL)

* For HighTide: *Ditch* (HighTide Festival 2010).
* Theatre includes: *In Celebration, Arcadia, Hamlet, Much Ado About Nothing, As You like It* (West End); *On the Ledge, Hinterland, Cripple of Inishmaan* (National Theatre); *The Hostage, Shadow of a Gunman, Lovegirl, The Innocent* (RSC); *The Plough and the Stars* (Young Vic); *Juno and the Paycock* (Donmar); *Doubt* (Tricycle); *Summerfolk, Saturday Sunday Monday* (Chichester Festival Theatre); *Death and the Maiden* (Royal Court tour); *The Life of the World to Come* (Almeida); *All My Sons* (Liverpool Rep); *Experiment with an Airpump* (Manchester Royal Exchange); *Dancing at Lughnasa, Juno and the Paycock, Touch of the Poet* (Broadway); *Cripple of Inishmaan* (Atlantic Theater NY and Geffen Theater LA).
* TV includes: *Wallander; U B Dead; Touch of Frost; Last Detective; Waking the Dead; Foyle's War; Midsomer Murders; Coronation Street; 55 Degrees North; Stan; New Tricks; Sex in the City; Proof; Romeo and Juliet; GBH; The Fragile Heart.*
* Film includes: *The Damned United; Blackwater Lightship; Home for Xmas; Tara Road; Bloom; This is the Sea; Frankie Starlight; Run of the Country; Taffin; Loade.*
* Awards: Drama Desk Award (2), Theatre World Special Award, London Critics Award, Irish Theatre Award (2), US Audi Award. Nominations: Tony Award, Irish Film and Television Award, Royal Television Society Award, Grammy Award.
* Dearbhla is an Associate Artist of the Abbey Theatre, the National Theatre of Ireland

PAUL RATTRAY (BUG)

Trained at Drama Centre London.
* For HighTide: *Ditch* (HighTide Festival 2010).
* Other theatre includes: *The Shawl* (Arcola Theatre); *Black Watch* (National Theatre of Scotland); *The Long and The Short and The Tall* (Crucible Theatre); *East Coast Chicken Supper* (Traverse Theatre); *In the Blue* (Theatre 505 / Young Vic); *Cool Water Murder* (Belgrade); *The Anatomist* (Edinburgh Lyceum); *Hand Bag* (ATC / Lyric Hammersmith); *Wolfskin* (Hardware); *Playing the Game* (Edinburgh Festival); *Decky Does a Bronco* (Grid Iron Theatre); *Dinner* (National Theatre).
* Television includes: *Doctors; Casualty; Last Rights; The Bill; Simple Things; Wet Work*
* Film includes: *Creep; Mike Bassett England Manager; Morvern Callar; Enigma; Max; Furnished Room; Night Sweeper.*
* Radio includes: *Black Watch* (BBC).

DANNY WEBB (BURNS)

* For HighTide: *Ditch* (HighTide Festival 2010).
* Other theatre includes: *Piano Forte* (Royal Court); *The Philanthropist* (Donmar Warehouse); *The Green Man* (Bush Theatre, London and The Drum, Plymouth); *Richard III* (Crucible Sheffield); *One Flew Over The Cuckoo's Nest* (Number One Tour); *Art* (Wyndham Theatre); *Trade* (Royal Court); *Blue Bird* (Royal Court); *Popcorn* (Apollo Theatre); *Goldhawk Road* (Bush Theatre); *Dead Funny* (Hampstead & Vaudeville); *Search and Destroy* (Royal Court Upstairs); *Death and The Maiden* (Duke of York); *Back Up The Hearse* (Hampstead Theatre); *The Pool of Bethesda* (Orange Tree, Richmond); *Hamlet* (Old Vic / Leicester Haymarket); *Serious Money* (Royal Court & Broadway); *Night Must Fall* (Greenwich Theatre); *The Nest* (Bush Theatre); *Progress* (Lyric, Hammersmith); *The Gardens of England* (National Theatre); *As I Lay Dying* (National Theatre); *Murderers* (National Theatre); *California Dog Fight* (Bush Theatre); and *Up For None* (National Theatre Studio). Also seasons with Glasgow Citizens Theatre and Liverpool Playhouse.

* Television includes: *Holby City; Midsomer Murders; Hustle; In Dalston No-one Can Hear You Scream; Landgirls; The Bill; Trinity; Britannia High; Casualty; Most Sincerely; New Tricks; Lark Rise to Candleford; Honest; Bloodlines; Miss Marple; Rise and Fall of Rome; Doctor Who II; Inspector Linley; Nostradamus; Totally Frank; Hotel Babylon; Lewis; Heartbeat; A Touch Of Frost XII; Death Experience; Silent Witness; Waking The Dead; My Family Christmas Special; Uncle Adolf; Murder in Suburbia; Dogma 3: Repeat After Me; Pepys; Life Begins; Murder Squad; Henry VIII; Cutting It; The Hound of The Baskervilles; Torch; Outside The Rules; Shackleton; McCready and Daughter; Take Me; The Knock; Hawk; Harbour Lights; Dalziel and Pascoe; Frenchman's Creek; Venus Hunters; The Jump; Out of Hours; 2.4 Children; The Cleopatra Files; Disaster at The Mall; King of Chaos; A Perfect State; True Tilda; Sharman, Murder Most Horrid; Mrs Hartley and The Growth Centre; Sharman; Our Friends in The North; Cardiac Arrest; A Woman's Guide to Adultery; Comics (serial); Head Hunters; Poirot; Tales of Sherwood Forest;* and *Intimate Contact.*
* Film includes: *The Arbour; The Courageous Heart of Irena Sendler; Valkyrie; The Story of...; The Harvester; The Aryan Couple; Stealing Lives; The Upside Of Anger; Family Business; Shiner; In The Name Of Love; Still Crazy; Love and Death on Long Island; True Blue; Alien III; Robin Hood; Henry V; Defence of The Realm; Billy The Kid; The Green Baize Vampire; The Year of The Quiet Sun; The Unapproachable; No Exit.*

COMPANY

BETH STEEL (WRITER)
Beth was born in Nottingham and was part of the Invitation Group for Emerging Writers at the Royal Court and is currently a writer on attachment for both HighTide and Theatre503. *Ditch* is her first play.

STEVEN ATKINSON (PRODUCER)
Training: BA Hons Film & Theatre, Reading University, and Assistant Director at Shakespeare's Globe.
* For HighTide: as Director; *Lidless* (HighTide Festival 2010, Edinburgh Festival); *Muhmah* (HighTide Festival 2009) and *The Pitch* (Latitude Festival). As Producer; *Stovepipe* (HighTide/National Theatre/Bush Theatre); *I Caught Crabs in Walberswick* (HighTide/Edinburgh Festival/Bush Theatre); *HighTide Festivals 2008, 2009, 2010.*
* Other Directing includes: *Freedom Trilogy* (Hull Truck); *Sexual Perversity in Chicago* (Edinburgh Festival).
* Awards include SOLT Stage One Bursary for New Producers. What's On Stage Award nomination for Best Off-West End Production (*Stovepipe*).
* Steven joined HighTide in 2007 and is the Artistic Director and Chief Executive. In 2006 aged 22, he was appointed as the first Literary Manager of Hull Truck Theatre.

ANDREA FERRAN (ASSISTANT DIRECTOR)
Training: Andrea received her MFA in Theatre Directing from Columbia University, New York
* Directing credits include: *Romeo and Juliet* (Bechstein Hall/Old Vic New York); *The Woman*; *Secret Life of the Office Worker* (Riverside Church, NY); *Mad Forest*; *Have I None; The Cherry Orchard* (Schapiro Theatre, NY); *Dr Faustus*, (Oxford Fire Station Theatre); *Conversations after a Burial;* Llosa's *La Chunga* (Burton Taylor Theatre).

Upcoming in 2010: *Fen* (Rose Theatre Studio, Kingston) and the UK Premiere of Philip Glass's Opera *Les Enfants Terribles* at the Arcola Theatre, London.

In 2008, Andrea co-founded VOLTA, a theatre company dedicated to contemporary ensemble work. In 2009, she received a directing fellowship from the Kennedy Centre, Washington DC. She has also trained with Théâtre du Soleil, The Living Theatre, Teatr Piesn Kozla and SITI Company and assisted Andrei Serban, Robert Woodruff, Shen Wei and Natalie Abrahami at Lincoln Center Theatre, Carnegie Hall, La Mama ETC and The Gate Theatre.

SAMUEL HODGES (PRODUCER)
* For HighTide: As actor – *Assembly/Lyre* (HighTide Festival 2007); as Producer – twelve productions, including *Stovepipe* (HighTide Festival 2008/ W12 Shopping Centre in association with the National Theatre and Bush Theatre); *I Caught Crabs in Walberswick* (HighTide Festival 2008/ Edinburgh Festival/ Bush Theatre).
* Other theatre includes: *The Winslow Boy* (Salisbury Playhouse); *A Man for All Seasons* (York Theatre Royal); *Men Without Shadows*; (Finborough Theatre); *Anatol* (Arcola Theatre); *The Fall of the House of Usher* (Etcetera Theatre and Cambridge Playrooms).
* Television includes: *Broadside*; *Doctors*; *Cambridge Spies*.

* Film includes: *Jane Eyre* (Ruby Films/BBC) and *Player* (writer, actor and producer).
* Awards include: SOLT Stage One Bursary for New Producers 2008, Best Short Film Nominations (*Player*) at Raindance, Miami and St Petersburg Film Festivals. Sam is the founder and Artistic Director of HighTide, and works as an actor, producer and writer.
* Samuel founded HighTide in 2006 and is Artistic Director.

TOM MILLS (MUSIC)
Training: Creative Music Technology at Bath Spa University, graduating in 2002.
* For HighTide: *Lidless* (HighTide Festival 2010, Edinburgh Festival); *Moscow Live* (HighTide Festival 2010)
* As a musical director and composer he has produced: *Breathing Irregular* and *The Kreutzer Sonata* (Gate Theatre); *The Jungle Book, The Grimm Brothers' Circus* and *Metropolis* (The Egg, Bath). As a composer and sound designer: *The Eternal Not* (National Theatre); *Edward Gant's Amazing Feats of Loneliness* (Headlong); *Unbroken* (Gate Theatre); *Othello* (Assembly Rooms, Bath); *Assassins* (Eyebrow Productions). As an actor musician: *The Good Person of Szechwan* and *The Berlin Cabaret* (Theatre Royal, Bath). As musical director: *Return to the Forbidden Planet* (Bath Spa Music Society); *Band of Blues Brothers* (Papillion Theatre Company). Upcoming projects include *Elektra* (Young Vic) and *Macbeth* (Regent's Park Open Air Theatre).
* Tom is also a producer and session musician mainly playing with *Passenger* and *Bridie King and the Reasons*.

MATT PRENTICE (LIGHTING)
Trained at Bristol Old Vic.
* For HighTide: *Stovepipe* (HighTide Festival 2008, National Theatre, Bush Theatre), *I Caught Crabs in Walberswick* (HighTide Festival 2008 & Edinburgh Festival & Bush Theatre); *Switzerland* (HighTide Festival 2008); *Certain Dark Things* (HighTide Festival 2008); *Stovepipe* (HighTide Festival 2008); *Fixer* (HighTide Festival 2009); *Guardians* (HighTide Festival 2009); *Fixer* (HighTide Festival 2009); *Muhmah* (HighTide Festival 2009); *Ditch* (HighTide Festival 2010); *Lidless* (HighTide Festival 2010); *Moscow Live* (HighTide Festival 2010).
* Other theatre includes: *Parade* (South Side, Edinburgh); *A Chorus Line* (Shaw Theatre); *The House of Bernarda Alba* (The Players Theatre); *The Young People's Theatre Company Showcase* (Gielgud Theatre); *Faust* (Punchdrunk and the National Theatre) *Peter Pan* (The Assembly Room, Derby); *Masque of the Red Death* (Punchdrunk, BAC).
* Awards include: Best Production Design, Critics Circle Awards 2006 for *Faust*.
* Matt is Head of Lighting at the Royal Academy of Dramatic Art and was previously the Head of Lighting Design at the Mountview Academy of Theatre Arts.

NATE SENCE (PRODUCER)
Nate joined HighTide in March 2010 as its first Executive Director. Nate has worked in arts management since 2001, most recently as Producer for The Opera Group, which tours musical theatre and opera throughout the UK and internationally. For The Opera Group Nate has helped to deliver several major touring productions including the 2008 Evening Standard Best Musical production of *Street Scene*. Prior to moving to the UK Nate served as Associate Managing Director at the Tony Award-winning Alliance Theatre in Atlanta, Georgia.

Nate is a graduate of Florida State University's Theatre Management – Master of Fine Arts Programme, and The University of Oklahoma's Drama Department. He also worked as an arts coordinator and educator in the New York Public Schools System while attaining an MS Degree in Education from Brooklyn College.

CHRISTOPHER SHUTT (SOUND)

Training: Bristol Old Vic Theatre School.

* Work for the National includes *War Horse, White Guard, Really Old Like Forty Five, Burnt by the Sun, Mrs Affleck, Every Good Boy Deserves Favour, Gethsemane, The Hour We Knew Nothing of Each Other, Philistines, Happy Days* (also world tour), *Coram Boy* (also on Broadway), *A Dream Play, Measure for Measure, Mourning Becomes Electra, The PowerBook, Humble Boy, Play Without Words, Hamlet, Albert Speer, Not About Nightingales, Chips with Everything, The Homecoming* and *Machinal*. Work for Complicité includes *A Disappearing Number, The Elephant Vanishes, A Minute Too Late, Mnemonic, Noise of Time, Street of Crocodiles, Three Lives of Lucie Cabrol,* and *Caucasian Chalk Circle*. Other work includes *Piaf, Hecuba, The Man Who Had All The Luck* at the Donmar; *Judgment Day* at the Almeida; *Aunt Dan & Lemon* at the Royal Court; *All My Sons* on Broadway; *The Bacchae* and *Little Otik* for National Theatre of Scotland; *The Caretaker* at Sheffield Crucible and the Tricycle; *Moon for the Misbegotten* at the Old Vic and on Broadway; *King Lear, Much Ado About Nothing, King John, Romeo & Juliet* for the RSC; *Julius Caesar* at the Barbican; *Beyond the Horizon* and *Spring Storm* at the Royal & Derngate, Northampton, and *The Resistible Rise of Arturo Ui* in New York with Al Pacino and Steve Buscemi, music by Tom Waits.
* Radio includes *A Shropshire Lad, Tennyson's Maud, A Disappearing Number* and *After the Quake.*
* Twice awarded the New York Drama Desk Award for Outstanding Sound Design. Olivier Award Nominations for *Coram Boy, War Horse, Piaf and Every Good Boy Deserves Favour.*

TAKIS (DESIGNER)

* For HighTide: *Ditch* (HighTide Festival 2010); *Lidless* (HighTide Festival 2010); *Moscow Live* (HighTide Festival 2010); *Guardians* (HighTide Festival 2009); *Fixer* (HighTide Festival 2009); *Muhmah* (HighTide Festival 2009); *Stovepipe* (National Theatre 2009 & HighTide Festival 2008); *I Caught Crabs in Walberswick* (HighTide Festival 2008 & Edinburgh Festival & Bush Theatre); *Switzerland* (HighTide Festival 2008); *Certain Dark Things* (HighTide Festival 2008).
* Other theatre includes: *The Early Bird* (Finborough Theatre); *Signs of a Star Shaped Diva* (Theatre Royal Stratford East & National Tour); *The Marriage Bed* (Hong Kong Academy for Performing Arts/ NY Sanford Meisner Theatre); *Invasion* (Soho Theatre); *Scenes from the Big Picture* (RADA); *Marat/Sade* (Jermyn Street Theatre); *Sing Yer Heart Out for the Lads* (RADA); *Crazy Lady* (Drill Hall & Contact Theatre Manchester); *Nikolina* (Pleasance Courtyard, Edinburgh Festival Fringe); *Installation 496* (RADA); *Schweyk in the Second World War* (Theatre Duisburg); *Medea* (Ancient Greek Theatre of Syracusa).
* Installations/Site-specific productions include: *Forgotten Peacock* (Design Museum/The Brunswick); *The Tempest* (Hobbs Factory); *Goldfish* (Paris Fashion Week); *Mythological Installation Oedipus* (Museum of Contemporary Art, Bucharest); *Visual Performance in Baroque Spirit* (Venice Carnival).

* Music performances includes: *A Tale of Two Cities* (Theatre Royal Brighton), *Maria Callas – Vissi D'arte; Vissi D'amore* (Barbican); *Choruses: Eternal Service to Beauty* (Ancient Theatre of Epidaurus/ Frankfurt Opera House); *In the Light of the Night* (Ancient Theatre of Epidaurus); *Nikos Skalkotas: a Celebration* (Queen Elizabeth Hall). www.takis.info

JOHN TUCKER MA (VOICE)

John Tucker is a voice coach and singing teacher. In his London studio (*www.john-tucker.com*), his work with actors and singers includes Bishi, Emily Bruni, William Houston, Niall Macgregor, Sophie Okonedo, Beth Orton, Diana Quick, Toby Stephens and Indira Varma. John is on the teaching faculty at BADA and has also taught at Central, Drama Centre London and RADA. John has held the position of Voice Associate at HighTide since 2007. He is a member of the BVA and VASTA.

RICHARD TWYMAN (DIRECTOR)

For Hightide: *Ditch* (HighTide Festival 2010).
* Directing includes: *Henry IV Part II* (RSC/Roundhouse); *The Abandoned City* (Royal Court Int. Residency); *Architect and Emperor of Assyria* (Gate); *Brassed Off* (York Theatre Royal); *A Desire to Kill on the Tip of the Tongue* (Edinburgh Fringe); *Julius Caesar* (Guildhall); *Romeo and Juliet* (Ancient Odeon, Paphos).
* Richard was the Associate Director on the acclaimed RSC Histories Cycle (*Richard II, Henry IV Pt I, Henry V, Henry VI Pt I, II, III* and *Richard III*) which won Olivier Awards for Best Revival, Best Ensemble and Best Costume and the Evening Standard Editor's Choice Award.
* As Assistant Director: *Othello, Sejanus, Thomas More, Breakfast With Mugabe* (RSC/West End); *Just a Bloke* (Royal Court); *Mariana Pineda* (Gate).

 HighTide

The first **HighTide Festival** in **2007** premiered eight short plays written by Tom Basden, Steven Bloomer, Sarah Cuddon, Sam Holcroft, Matthew Morrison, Pericles Snowdon, Megan Walsh and Iain Weatherby.

Tom Basden's *Assembly* then transferred to Hay-on-Wye Festival 2008.

The second **HighTide Festival** in **2008** premiered four plays written by Adam Brace, Joel Horwood, Nick Payne and the fourth devised by You Need Me.

Joel Horwood's *I Caught Crabs in Walberswick* transferred to the Edinburgh Festival Fringe 2008, a UK tour, and The Bush Theatre, in a co-production with Eastern Angles.

Adam Brace's *Stovepipe* transferred to West 12 in London as a site-sympathetic production in collaboration with the National Theatre and Bush Theatre in March 2009.

Nick Payne's *The Pitch* premiered at Latitude Festival 2008, Suffolk.

The third **HighTide Festival** in **2009** premiered three plays written by Lydia Adetunji, Lucy Caldwell and Jesse Weaver.

Lydia Adetunji's *Fixer* and Adam Brace's *Stovepipe* transferred to the National Play Festival in Brisbane, Australia, in January 2010.

The fourth **HighTide Festival** in **2010** premiered three plays written by Serge Cartwright, Frances Ya-Chu Cowhig and Beth Steel.

Beth Steel's *Ditch* transferred to The Old Vic Tunnels in London, in a co-production with The Old Vic, in May 2010.

Frances Ya-Chu Cowhig's *Lidless* will transfer to HighTide City Wall at the Edinburgh Festival, as part of HighTide's programme *inFRINGEment*.

Tickets for *inFRINGEment* go on sale 1 June 2010
www.hightide.org.uk

FOR **HighTide**

24a St John Street,
London,
EC1M 4AY
0207 566 9765
www.hightide.org.uk
hello@hightide.org.uk

INTRODUCTION TO THE HIGHTIDE WAREHOUSE

The Warehouse is the umbrella name for the programmes through which HighTide
encourages individuals to become involved in our work.

GENESIS LABORATORY

HighTide's open-access Research and Development Studio based in London, providing
bursaries, space, and collaboration to emerging playwrights, directors, actors and companies,
supported by the Genesis Foundation.

RESIDENT PLAYWRIGHTS

HighTide's annual playwright residencies in which three writers per year, sourced through an
annual call for submissions, have one play fully produced and additional plays given further
development and support.

THE JOHN FERNALD ASSISTANT DIRECTOR AWARD

An annual bursary for three directors-in-training offering assisting roles in a HighTide Festival
production, the transfer, and the opportunity to direct in the Genesis Laboratory.

HIGHTIDE ENSEMBLE

The HighTide Ensemble of actors with whom HighTide works around the year, starting with
the festival productions, and including each transfer, stand-alone productions, and
residencies, laboratories and readings.

FIRST LOOK

HighTide's work with young people aged 13 - 21 in Suffolk, aimed at demystifying the process
of theatre-making for the future generations of theatre practitioners.

STILL ACTIVE

HighTide's arts management training programme for elderly residents in east Suffolk who
help to manage and deliver the annual HighTide Festival in Suffolk

For more details and how to apply please visit www.hightide.org.uk

HighTide presents

inFRINGEment

Impressions on Oppression: A programme of work

at HighTide City Wall (Venue 146)

LIDLESS
a new play by Frances Ya-Chu Cowhig.
19:30 daily (except 17th August)

"An extraordinary and original attempt to show the enduring strain on the victims of torture in Guantanamo." David Hare

NOTES FROM A CELL, a series of reactions to the loss of civil liberty. From emerging and leading playwrights around the world. **13.00 daily**

FILMS FOR FREE, a programme of night-time screeners. Featuring feature films, shorts, and documentaries every night. **22:00 daily**

HighTide
www.hightide.org.uk

UNDERBELLY ESCALATOR

ideas tap

LOTTERY FUNDED

THE OLD VIC

The Old Vic's iconic building has a rich history of great productions and performances from Laurence Olivier's Hamlet to Ian McKellen's Widow Twankey. Under the artistic leadership of Kevin Spacey, The Old Vic continues to attract the best creative talent.

Through Old Vic New Voices, The Old Vic also nurtures young actors, writers and directors, and works with schools and our neighbours to bring theatre to a wider audience.

In February 2010, The Old Vic acquired a lease for a subterranean series of tunnels from British Rail and a premises licence from Lambeth Council, to create a performance space beneath Waterloo Station. The Old Vic Tunnels will showcase productions, performances and installations and will be home to a series of innovative and surprising arts events throughout 2010.

Ditch by Beth Steel is an Old Vic co-production with HighTide in The Old Vic Tunnels.

Production Acknowledgements:
Project Manager for The Old Vic Tunnels: Douglas McJannet
Press Agent for The Old Vic: Jo Allan PR
Photographer for The Old Vic Tunnels: Matt Humphrey
Insurance: Walton & Parkinson

Ditch

For Mum and Dad

Setting
The Peak District. The future.

Characters
Both the women and men appear older than their given ages, due to labour in harsh weather and lost years.

Mrs Peel, *fifty-eight years old.*
Megan, *twenty years old.*
Burns, *early fifties.*
Bug, *late thirties.*
Turner, *late thirties.*
James, *twenty years old.*

Production note
The entire stage is to be covered thickly in barren peat. The peat should rise around the perimeter of the stage to create a shallow ditch where the action takes place. The peat is there to be interacted with, which is to say, as the characters rise and fall they will be covered in dirt.

Act One

Scene One

A remote farm, now a Security outpost in the Peak District. Plot of land. Early evening, the light is fading fast. The guttural croak of a raven overhead. Dogs bark.

Turner (*Off stage.*)   Woo-Hoo!

Turner *runs out followed by* **James**.

Turner (*Hollers out.*)   You jammy cunt! He gonna be gloatin' all night.

James   Where's he takin' her?

Turner   Putting her in that outbuildin' over there. I been one ahead, now she makes us even.

James   You keep a score?

Turner   Aint as if it's every day yer getting' one. That's the first Illegal we picked up in six weeks.

James   What a' you doin' the rest a' the time?

Turner   Tuggin' our dicks. Out lookin' for the next ones s'what we doin'.

Turner *takes out his flask, belts back a drink.*

Most a' the time me and Bug over there a' out patrollin' together. But I'll have you with me for a few days, train you up and then you can go out with Burns.

James   Been given a letter for him.

Turner   Letter? How'd you get it?

James   Headquarters in Manchester.

Turner   You got it with yer now?

James *nods.*

Turner   Let me have a look at it.

James   It sealed.

Turner   Aint gonna open it.

James   S'what you want it for?

Turner   Just give me the fuckin' letter.

James *produces the letter.* **Turner** *snatches looks at the envelope.*

Turner   Shit.

James   What?

Turner   Can't tell what's in it.

Turner *gives the envelope to* **James**.

Turner   Burns's boy, Brian, been deployed three year ago.

James   Thinkin' he dead?

Turner   Probably says he comin' back, now that we got the strong hold over there.

Bug *enters jauntily.*

Bug   What'd you say to that then?

Turner   Yeah, alright. This here is big useless Greg.

James *and* **Bug** *shake hands.*

Bug   Bug.

James   James.

Bug   A we glad to see you.

James   Glad to be here.

Bug   They gettin' younger or we older?

Turner   Good to see 'em signin' up.

Bug   They been sayin' they gonna send us more men for two months.

James   Well I'm just the one.

Bug   It's somethin'.

Turner   Things a' lookin' up.

Bug   What time you get here?

Turner   About an hour ago.

Bug   Alright, aint it?

James   Glad to be here.

Bug   Where you been posted before?

James   London.

Bug (*Laughs.*)   I bet yer fuckin' are.

Turner (*Laughs.*)   What a shit hole eh?

Turner and **Bug** *are now quiet.*

Bug   It the way they say?

James   I guess.

Bug   You ain't sure?

James   Never knowed what it like before.

Turner   London's finished.

Bug   No sign a' Recovery there?

Turner   What's it matter?

Bug   Bein' London an' all.

Turner   Manchester's where it's at now.

Bug   Yeah, I know.

Turner   Been improvements there.

Bug   Just askin'.

Turner   Where'd you pick her up?

Bug   About twenty mile from the Sheffield border.

Turner   She have a bag with her?

Bug   Nothin'.

Turner   You pick up a woman with no bag, means she up the spout.

James   You get many that way?

Turner   More than you'd think.

Bug   Them rods in 'em aint guaranteed.

Turner   Dint show up at a clinic or ripped 'em out.

James   Where's she go from here?

Bug   Take her to the train station.

Turner   Same you got off earlier.

Bug   Burns back?

Turner   Nah, better be back here soon, I'm champin' at the bit for tonight.

Bug   Now we got two things to celebrate.

Turner   You comparin' seizin' a knocked-up Illegal to seizin' a pipeline?

Bug *sheepishly shakes his head.*

Turner   Tonight's about the man that had the bollocks to go over there, and had the bollocks to fight. (*Raises his flask.*) We celebratin' the King's bollocks.

Turner *and* **Bug** *belt one back.*

James   Where we goin'?

Bug   When?

James   Tonight? To celebrate.

Turner *and* **Bug** *laugh.*

Turner   Aint goin' nowhere. This here. (*Stops laughing.*) This is your world. Entire. Sky.

Bug   Mountains.

Turner   Moors.

Bug   Bogs.

Turner   Mud.

Bug   Dirt.

Turner   Cuckoo spit.

Bug   Fox piss.

Turner   Dog shit.

Bug   Cow shit.

Turner   Horse shit.

Bug   Stage skunk.

Turner   And fuck all else.

Burns **enters.**

Turner (*To* **Bug**.)   He's thinkin' about how he can laid already.

Burns   Welcome to the Peak.

Burns *and* **James** *shake hands.*

Burns   Burns.

James   James.

Burns   Just got in?

James   Bout an hour ago.

Burns   How was the train up here?

James   Took a while.

Burns   Been some time since I travelled about.

Burns   What's it lookin' like?

James   What d'you mean?

Burns   See any construction work goin' on?

Bug   She in the outbuildin'.

James   Can't say I did.

Burns   Buildin' a homes?

James *shakes his head.*

Turner   He only been sat on a train.

Burns   Repairin' a' roads?

James *shakes his head.*

Turner   Arterial roads have been fixed.

Burns   Nothin' like that?

James *shakes his head.*

Burns   No sign a' Recovery then?

Turner   Priorities s'what they been doin'.

Burns   Thought the Recovery was one.

Beat.

Bug   I got an Illegal.

Burns   Wasn't expectin' yer till tomorrow.

James   When I got inta Manchester there been a freight leavin' early, so I took that.

Burns   Been over to Headquarters whilst you there.

James   Been given a letter for yer.

Burns   Letter? What kind a' letter?

James *produces the letter.* **Burns** *takes it and reads the envelope.* **James** *steps away.* **Turner** *nods at* **Bug** *for them to give* **Burns** *some space.* **Burns** *opens the envelope and reads the letter. Pause. He laughs. The men turn round.*

Burns   I been put in charge.

Bug *and* **James** *happily step forwards.* **Turner** *stays where he is with a face like a smacked arse.*

Bug (*Pats back.*) Congratulations.

James (*Shakes hand.*) Congratulations.

Turner What's it say?

Burns You can read it later.

Turner Like to read it now.

Burns It goin' up on the kitchen wall.

Mrs Peel *enters.*

Mrs Peel She's pregnant and she far gone.

Bug She aint showin'. You checked?

Mrs Peel She as wide as a river in spate.

Bug (*Grins.*) Nothin' worse.

Mrs Peel When yer boat aint big enough.

Mrs Peel *leaves.*

Burns There's a train leavin' at eleven. (*To* **Bug**.) You'll just about make it.

Turner We celebratin' tonight.

Burns Next trains not for a week.

Turner What difference does it make?

Burns No need to drag this thing out.

Turner Aint as if she gonna drop it in a week.

Burns Best she goes now.

Turner He aint gonna get back here till gone three.

Burns Put her on a horse too.

Turner I say we vote on it.

Burns I say what goes on around here now.

Bug *nods,* **Turner** *nods grudgingly.* **Burns** *leaves.*

Bug   He just pissed all over my strawberries.

Bug *leaves.* **Turner** *and* **James** *watch him go.*

Turner   There's no way Stevens would a' done that.

James   Who's Stevens?

Turner   He the boss round here.

James   Where'd he go?

Turner   Venezuela, with the rest a' 'em. There been eight a' us here to start with.

Turner *walks off in the opposite direction to* **Bug**.

Turner (*Stops.*)   You comin'? (*Storms off.*) We got a war victory to celebrate.

James *leaves.*

Scene Two

Kitchen. Afternoon.

Megan *has mopped the floor, she now rings out the mop.* **James** *enters stops as he sees the wet floor between the two of them.*

James   Mornin'.

Megan *spins round.*

Megan   Mornin'.

James   Guess I can't come in here.

They look at the floor . . .

James   How long it gonna take to dry?

Megan   Five minutes.

James   Five?

Megan   Three, maybe.

James   Hard to be exact.

Megan   It tricky to judge.

James   I bet.

They look at each other . . .

James   Come back in five then.

James *makes to leave.*

Megan   Bound to be three by now.

James   Don't seem worth goin'.

Megan   Just to come back again.

Beat.

Megan   You could wait here?

James   I'm not botherin' you?

Megan   I just finished. Well . . . almost.

Megan's *eyes narrow on a supposed blemish on the floor.*

Megan   Missed a bit.

Megan *takes steps forwards with the mop.*

James   It's Megan?

Megan *abandons the idea of mopping.*

Megan   Yeah.

They move towards one another almost imperceptibly.

James   I'm –

Megan   James.

James   Yeah.

They smile, look down at the floor and edge back again in embarrassment.

Megan   What you come here for?

James   Boilin' water. Thought I'd have a shave.

Megan   When's your birthday?

James   Twelfth a' April.

Megan   Just passed.

James *nods.*

Megan   Shame.

James   Why's that?

Megan   You get a bath on your birthday. I had mine too, tenth a' January.

Beat.

Megan   I spent the whole evenin' in mine. Must a' been in it for five hours. Mrs Peel kept bringin' me more hot water each time it went cold and by the end a' it the bath was so full it covered every inch a' me. Then I did somethin' I never done before, to make it special. I opened my eyes in the water, like I was swimmin'. And then, at the very end, I put a jug a' milk in it. (*Shrugs.*) Made my tits soft.

Mrs Peel *enters. She glares at them.*

Megan   He just waitin' for the floor to dry.

Mrs Peel   Looks bone dry to me.

Megan   I'll put that pan a' water on.

James   I'll come back later.

James *makes to leave.*

Mrs Peel   Before you do I'm gonna say a few things about the handlin' a this place that we women see too. Burns may a' told you some a' this already but I'm gonna say it anyway. Cause I like to tell it and Megan here, she like to hear it.

First off. We got plenty to do around here. There aint no idle time for me and her till I give it, aint that right Megan?

Megan *nods.*

Mrs Peel   We got livestock to see to, cleanin' to be done, and meals to be made. You get your breakfast, one cup a' coffee and the pleasure a' me in here at eight. You campin' out and need some food with yer, you come to me about it. Otherwise you get your dinner in here at seven at and it'll be served by *me*. You like deer?

James *opens his mouth to speak* …

Mrs Peel   Cause it's gonna come fried, boiled, smoked, roasted, dried, burnt and raw. (*Lowers her gaze to his groin.*) Every a' inch a' it too. I don't do requests or suggestions, come dinner you get what you get. Same as outside we get toiletry supplies once a month. I recommend you use two sheets a' paper for a piss and three for a shit. We don't grow toilet paper, when it's gone it's gone. Any questions?

Mrs Peel's *eyes narrow onto* **James** *frame.*

Mrs Peel   You're gonna need to thicken up for the winter. We feel it out here, gets inta your bones, worth it for the clean air though. I'll see to it that I skim the butterfat, get plenty of milk in yer.

James   How'd yer get fresh milk?

Mrs Peel   From a cow's tit.

James   Aint had fresh milk since I been a kid.

Mrs Peel   We set up alright here.

James   You must a' had a farm or somethin' before?

Mrs Peel   There's one more thing for me to tell and I only gonna say it once. I've listened to all the stories a' my generation, then watched 'em get sick or fade away. And it wasn't this world that killed 'em. It was the other. The memory of it. Now. I'm fifty eight, still standin', with nothin' more than a bit a' ring worm. We don't talk about the past here.

Mrs Peel *stares at* **James**. **James** *leaves quietly*. **Megan** *rushes to the stove*.

Mrs Peel   What a' you doin'?

Megan   He forgot the water.

Mrs Peel   He dint forget. He decided he dint want it after all.

Mrs Peel *glares at* **Megan**. **Burns** *enters*.

Burns   Mornin'.

Mrs Peel   Afternoon.

Burns   Suppose it is. We kept yer awake last night?

Mrs Peel   Nothin' disturbs my beauty sleep.

Burns   Cause us men were goin' for it.

Mrs Peel   That aint kept me awake yet.

Burns *sits and picks horse shit off his boot,* **Megan** *watches it fall to the floor.*

Burns   How long for that deer?

Mrs Peel   It aint bled out yet.

Burns   Couple a' hours?

Mrs Peel   I gotta gut her too.

Burns   Three yer say?

Mrs Peel   Then I gotta skin her.

Burns   How long?

Mrs Peel   Four, butcherin's hard work.

Burns   Wanted the boy to have some meat 'for he goes out.

Mrs Peel   Got some dried arse rashers.

Burns   That the best you can do? Still, better than what everyone else has. Can I get a tea?

Megan *looks up from the floor and prepares the tea.*

Mrs Peel   It better, but we could have more.

Mrs Peel *brings out a potato from her apron.*

Mrs Peel (*Sniffs with pride.*)   Now there's this here tater.

Burns *stands,* **Megan** *rushes over,* **Mrs Peel** *guards her potato jealously.*

Mrs Peel   It early, but it right enough.

Megan   I can smell it.

Burns   I can taste it.

Megan   We gonna roast 'em?

Burns   We havin' em mashed.

Megan   Mashed taters and deer!

Burns   How many a' down there?

Mrs Peel   This is it.

Beat.

Burns   You sown one tater?

Mrs Peel   It the only 'en to survive.

Burns *and* **Megan** *walk away.*

Mrs Peel   This here's, the beginnin'.

Burns *sits down.*

Mrs Peel   If I can get one I can get more. That plot a' land by the stables, that's the sod I sown this in. That sod would yield a crop.

Burns   We an outpost here, Mrs Peel. Not a farm.

Mrs Peel   Most a' the works preparin' the land, but then we'd be set.

Burns   Need a plough to do that.

Mrs Peel   Spades'd do the work of a plough, could get some vegetable plots out a' it too.

Burns   You and Megan'd be spadin' for weeks.

Mrs Peel   Can't wait that long, humidity'll get em like it done before. If we had some extra hands with us . . .

Burns   I aint puttin' my men on a shovel.

Mrs Peel   Me and her'd tend to it after that. Barn's good for storin' what we'd harvest.

Burns   I aint sayin' it again.

Mrs Peel   We could be self sufficient, no more tinned rations.

Burns   Answers no.

Pause. **Mrs Peel** *brings out the potato and rubs it.*

Mrs Peel   See how the skin's comin' off?

Burns doesn't look at Mrs Peel.

Mrs Peel   Skin aint had the chance to set firm.

Mrs Peel *sets the potato on the table before* **Burns**.

Mrs Peel   Means it's new.

Turner, *worse for wear, and* **Bug** *enter.*

Mrs Peel   Brand new.

Burns *now looks at the potato.*

Turner   I got a head as bad as a bastard. Coffee on?

Megan   Doin' it now.

Bug   Is that a spud?

Turner   Need somethin' to settle my gut.

Bug   How come we've got spuds?

Megan   Fetch you some milk?

Turner *ignores* **Megan**'s *offer and looks at the potato on the table.*

Turner   Fried taters.

Turner *turns to* **Bug**.

Bug   Fried deer.

Bug *turns to* **Turner**.

Turner   Fried egg.

Bug   Tin a' beans.

The realisation hits them at the same time.

Bug   That's a full English breakfast!

Turner   Kiss me quick I'm comin'!

Mrs Peel   Tater aint for breakfast.

Mrs Peel *shoves the potato in her apron.*

Turner   Why, what a' we havin'?

Mrs Peel   I make it way past eight.

Turner   I make it your job to cater for us.

Beat. **Mrs Peel** *lights the stove.*

Bug   Where's James?

Turner   He up and around.

Bug   Shall I go get him?

Turner   What a' you askin' me for?

Bug *walks out of the kitchen.*

Bug (*Hollers.*)   James! . . . (*Hollers.*) James! . . . (*Hollers.*) James!

Bug *comes back into the kitchen.*

Turner   I got a tongue as dry as a horse's hoof, that coffee ready?

Megan   Bringin' it now.

Megan *brings the coffee to the table as* **James** *enters.*

Bug (*To* **James**.)   Breakfast.

James   Thought I'd missed it.

James *sits at the table.*

Bug   Slept well?

James   Yeah, I did.

Turner   With them dogs barkin'?

James   Too tired to hear anythin'.

Turner   You must a' heard 'em, Burns?

Burns   What?

Turner   Dogs goin' at it last night. I say we head over to Edale, pitch up there for a couple a' days.

Bug *agrees.*

James   Where's Edale?

Turner   North east a' here, about twenty mile. Nothin' to it really, just a straight mile a' cottages runnin' through.

Bug   It been empty a long time, way before the orders came to leave. Been a tourist spot before, droves a' walkers passin' through on weekends, kind a' place southerners retired too.

Turner   What it is is a prime spot for Illegals.

Bug   We check the cottages for any sign a' 'em, blankets, smuts still alive, empty tinned food cans where the sauce aint turned.

Turner   They hole up in 'em before makin' their way just north a' there to the Pennine Way, leads all the way up to the Scottish border. Most a' the time that's where the cunts a' headin', Scotland.

Bug   Thinkin' it better in the north.

Turner   Sometimes I reckon the border restrictions should be lifted for a week.

Mrs Peel *and* **Megan** *bring in four plates of a dismal breakfast.*

Turner   Let all the Civilians in cities and settlements go where ever the fuck they want and see it pretty much the same everywhere. After that they'd be back in their pens and the cunts'd stay put, no more Illegals. (*Grins with a mouthful.*) But then we'd be out of a' job.

Beat.

Turner   That alright with you Burns if we do Edale?

Burns (*Nods.*)   Do a circle on the way back by Kinder Scoutt.

Turner   You takin' James out with you or he comin' with us?

Burns   Me and him's stayin' about here.

Turner   Showed him what there is yesterday.

Burns   There's some work to be done.

Turner   What work?

Burns   Seein' to that plot a' land by the stables.

Mrs Peel *looks over at* **Burns** *and* **Turner** *sees her.*

Burns   Preparin' it for a crop.

Bug   More spuds?

Burns   Needs to be weeded and spaded first.

Bug   All a' it?

Burns   Me and James'll start her off.

Bug   That's a lot a' shovellin'.

Burns   Youse can take over when you get back, be done in a week or so.

Turner *stands.*

Bug   Where you goin'?

Turner   To do my job.

Turner *walks off.* **Bug** *stands.*

Burns   See you in a couple a' days.

Bug *nods and leaves.*

Burns   Any good at shovellin' James?

James   Can't say I done it before.

Mrs Peel *enters to clear the plates.*

Burns   S'like bein' the batsman in cricket.

James   Can't say I been that either.

Burns *and* **James** *leave.*

Burns   It's all in the kneel.

Mrs Peel   Burns?

Burns *stops before he leaves turns to* **Mrs Peel**. *Beat.*

Mrs Peel   New boy been in here this mornin'. He been real excited to know we got a cow, way I see it he aint had his hands around a teat in a long time. Make sure he knows that milkin' the cow aint his job round here.

Mrs Peel *leaves.*

Scene Three

Peak. Night.

Turner *is sat staring into the small fire.* **Bug** *approaches* **Turner** *from behind. The horses are heard to stir occasionally.*

Bug (*Sheepishly.*)   Turner . . .

Turner   What?

Beat.

Turner   What you forgot this time?

Bug   The tarp.

Turner   What a' we gonna do now?

Bug   We could go back?

Turner   I aint goin' back.

Bug   I could go back.

Turner   Fuck the tarp.

Bug   Fuck the tarp?

Turner   Fuck the tarp. Fuck the rain. Fuck the land. Fuck Burns.

Bug (*Grins.*)   Thought you was pissed at me.

Turner   And fuck you.

Bug (*Still grinning.*)   But you aint.

Turner   Aint you pissed about it?

Bug   Yeah, I'm pissed. But. Way I see it, I only gotta be pissed for three days.

Turner   Three days?

Bug   Four max.

Turner   We supposed to be patrollin' this here bastard peak, and now there's just two a' us doin' it.

Bug   We'll be four by the end a' the week.

Turner   By then we could a' lost out on god knows how many Illegals.

Bug   Aint as if we pickin' 'em up every week, Turn.

Turner   You know why? Cause they fear us. They fear us, Bug. That's why.

Bug *looks out.*

Turner   This whole gardenin' thing, it dint come from Burns.

Bug   What d'you mean?

Turner   That old rope, Peel. It her idea.

Bug   Wouldn't mind havin' some spuds.

Turner   She sowin' more than that.

Bug   Reckon we'll get peas?

Turner   Would you stop thinkin' about your gut and think about what's goin' on here. Aint Burns puttin' us on a shovel, it Peel, a civilian. I like Burns, don't get me wrong, he been a good soldier, done his fair share a' tours. But that was some time ago, this last three year he been lookin' up at the moon through a whiskey bottle waitin' for his boy to come back. He aint got the grit to do the job, s'all I'm sayin'.

Beat.

Turner   Put some food on?

Bug   Aint hungry yet.

Turner   Me neither

Bug   You know what I been thinkin' about?

Turner   Gettin' laid?

Bug   Yeah, but soemthin' else too.

Turner *looks blank.*

Bug   Keep thinkin' about that stag.

Turner   Why?

Bug   I don't know.

Turner   So what you talkin' about it for?

Bug   I don't know.

Beat.

Bug   Never seen a stag bitten like that.

Turner   Seen it before.

Bug   Whatever it was knew what it was doin', straight for the jugular.

Turner   What d'you mean: whatever it was?

Bug   I don't know.

Turner   Told you a dog done it.

Bug   It was a big bastard too.

Turner   Fuckin' three dogs then.

Bug   Not an organ left.

Turner   How many times has one of them stray dogs come at you? Them dogs have spent most a' their life sprawled on a rug in front of a TV fartin'. But with all that gone they're wild.

Bug   Yeah, you're right.

Beat.

Bug   Never seen a dog this far inta the Peak.

Turner   And I never had such a borin' conversation.

Beat.

Bug   Haven't pitched in this spot for a while.

Turner   Couple a' week maybe.

Bug   Had this dream, last time we were sleepin' here. Not really a dream cause I was awake, sleepy eyed kind a' thing. The whole place was lit. Burnin'. Red with fire. Some trees fallin'. The ground scorched . . .

Turner   And then what?

Bug (*Shrugs.*)   Nothin'.

Scene Four

Stables. Evening.

Megan *is laid on her back staring upwards.* **James** *enters.*

James   Evenin'.

Megan *jumps to her feet.*

Megan   Evenin'.

James   Came to check the tack for my horse.

Megan   Which one been given?

James   Sheets.

Beat.

James   What a' you doin'?

Megan   I'm bein' alone.

Beat.

James   You come here to do that?

Megan   Huhum.

Beat.

Megan   Mrs Peel don't tend to come here. She don't like the horses much, especially Mince. He been eating her sage bush. Sheets kicked her in the gut. But she was alright about that.

James   Guess I'll be goin' then.

Megan   I don't mind sharin' this space. I could just sit here alone, sit here sharin' it, s'all the same to me – you like stars?

James   I guess.

Megan   Want a' see some?

James   Alright.

Megan   S'why I'm always in this spot so I can see 'em.

James *edges forwards to where* **Megan** *stands.*

Megan   I sometimes sit outside when you all sleepin' and look at 'em too. It's so quiet and dark. Never no planes in the sky, no headlights, lights from windows. Just them stars and me. You know that the stars a' suns?

James *shakes his head.*

Megan   Suns just the closet one to us is all. Mrs Peel told me that. Told me that everyone a' them stars is gonna die sometime and same goes for ours. But before it dies, a long time before it dies, it gonna cook us to a crisp and boil all the water away. You know that?

James *shakes his head.*

Megan   She told me that the moons done for too. Every year it moves further away and there'll come a time when it won't support us no more, we're gonna drop like a sack a' taters. You know that?

James *shakes his head.*

Megan   Don't really matter anyway cause the sun'll cook us first.

Beat.

James   Know how to find the North star.

Megan   Mrs Peel don't know that.

James   There's seven bright stars in the shape of a saucepan. You find the saucepan and take the edge a' it that's furthest away from the handle. You draw a line from the star at the base a' the pan to the star at the rim. You extend it about five times. That leads you to another saucepan. A smaller one. You take the edge a' the smaller saucepan's handle that's furthest away from the pan and you found the North Star. Drop a vertical line from the North Star to the horizon and that's north.

Megan *is lost yet impressed.*

James   Orientation was part a' my trainin'. Taught to orientate ourselves without a compass. Had to learn to memorize co-ordinates. Told never to fold a map any other way than it already folded. That way you give nothin' about the operation away. I liked that part a' it, learnin' I mean.

Megan   How much schoolin' you had?

James   Till I was twelve.

Megan   Same here.

James   We must be the same age then.

Megan   I like learnin' too.

Beat.

James   Show you some tactical hand signals if you want?

Megan   What a' they?

James   Stuff you do to not give the operation away.

Megan*'s game.*

James (*Raise his arm clenches his fist.*)   Hold.

Megan (*Does the same.*)   Hold.

James (*Crosses his arms across his chest.*)   Obstacle.

Megan (*Does the same.*)   Obstacle.

James (*Raises his arm, points the finger, rotates it.*)   Regroup.

Megan (*Does the same.*)   Regroup.

James (*Hand into a spy hole.*)   Look out.

Megan (*Does the same.*)   Look out.

James (*Cups his ear.*)   Say again.

Megan (*Does the same.*)   Say again.

James   Best stop there, gets confusin' if you do too many.

Megan   Never been someone my age here before.

James   Security's always been full a' the other generation. But since most a' thems gone overseas it left an openin' for us. Now that we old enough to do it. I signed up a year ago.

Beat.

Megan   So now you got health care.

James   Yeah. Not that I need it, I aint got nothin'.

Megan   Good to have it.

James   I guess.

Megan   Get more rations too.

James   When I was outside, here we eatin' the same.

Megan   Bigger livin' quarters for you.

James   Aint done it for none a' that.

Megan (*Nods.*)   Just wanted to be in the Security.

James   First time I had a choice in somethin'. Everythin' else been decided for me. Figured, if I'm gonna be drafted as well, I'd rather choose it then it get me. So that's what I done. Some a' them I knew dint speak to me after I done it. But. They don't speak much to each other outside anyway. This is the most I talked in a long time. Gonna get me in bother, like it did this mornin' with Mrs Peel.

Megan   She always like that.

James   Should a' known better.

Megan   Should be able to ask things sometimes.

The horses are heard to whinny. **Megan** *becomes alert.*

James   I should be goin'.

Megan   Probably just a mouse stirred 'em.

James   You sure Mrs Peel aint gonna come?

Megan   Last time I seen her she was pullin' whiskers out a' her chin and nose. She don't tend to come out a' our room after she been doin' that. This here's my free time, don't get much a' that.

James   She worked you hard on that shovel today.

Megan   She always workin' me, even when there's nothin' needs doin', but it good for me. When there was more men here I been busy most a' the time but when they went away I been told I was gonna be sent back to my old quarters and put to work in the refinery.

James   How come you stayed?

(*Beat.*)

Megan   Turner, he put in a good word for me.

James   Don't seem like him.

Megan   Here a bit like where I grew up, dint have horses a' nothin' but reminds me a' it sometimes . . .

James   Thought you dint talk about the past here?

Megan   I don't do everythin' Mrs Peel tells me. Today I chucked a handful a seeds down the toilet. Yesterday I tipped coffee grinds inta the compost like I been told too, but I slung in a tea bag, like I been told not too. Day before I spotted a hare munchin' away at her first ever courgette flower and I stood by and let it eat it down to the core. Last month I took a knife and made a gash in her mosquito nettin', and sure enough she been bit. And for a year I been watchin' a vine slowly spreadin' itself on top a' the spade I hid and I let it keep on growin' like toe nails on a corpse.

Burns (*Offstage.*)   James?

James   I gotta go.

Megan   He just callin' he aint comin' here.

Burns (*Offstage.*)   James?

James   I should go.

James *walks away, stops, turns around.*

James   Maybe see you in here again?

Megan   I don't mind sharin' this space.

Megan *sits.*

Megan   S'all same to me.

James *leaves.* **Megan** *smiles.*

Scene Five

Kitchen. Afternoon.

Mrs Peel *and* **Megan** *are before the table which is covered in seeds.* **James** *and* **Burns** *are bringing boxes of supplies into the kitchen.*

Mrs Peel   Potatoes, peas, beans are all the seed for their kind, cucumbers and most fruit contain the seed within 'em, we'll pick 'em out. Reason there's so many different kinds is, where one will fail another can still succeed. They're not all gonna' survive. Nature knows that, spreads it chances. When pickin' leaves and mushrooms you gotta be careful that they aint poisonous. A rule a' thumb I swear by is if you don't recognize it or it's got a dick don't trust it. (*Glares at* **James**.) Get rid a' it.

Burns *sits on a box and decanters the whiskey bottle into his flask.*

Mrs Peel (*To* **Burns**.)   One a' your dogs has been in here last night and had itself a free for all. I had a deer's tongue in a little dish over there, marinadin' in some vinegar and garlic over night –

Burns   Vinegar and garlic?

Mrs Peel   I don't appreciate feedback on my cookin'. I walk in here, dish is tipped over, and No Tongue. Best bit too.

Burns   Yer can say that again.

Mrs Peel *dislikes* **Burns**'s *tone and lets him know it.*

Burns   I'll tell 'em to be more careful when tyin' 'em up at night.

Mrs Peel   Damn good kick up the goolies is what it needs.

Burns   You got one less bag a' flour and no coffee.

Mrs Peel   You got tea?

Burns *nods.*

Mrs Peel   You checked it? Cause last time they diddled yer.

Burns   Everythin' else is there.

Mrs Peel *shifts her attention back to* **Megan**.

Mrs Peel   Most a' what you gonna be doin' is sowin', waterin' and harvestin'. But you'll need to have the eye a' the hawk about you at all times. Why? Cause you're on the look out for Fungus . . .

James *enters with the last of the supplies.*

Mrs Peel   And he comes in all shapes and guises. Mould, mildew, black spot. You see any sign a' Fungus you come to me.

James *looks at the seeds on the table.*

Mrs Peel   You see a bird pullin' at the tops a' my spring opinions, a hare helpin' itself to my cabbages, a slug suckin' up my salad (*turns on* **James**) what d'you do?

James   I come to you?

Mrs Peel   Wrong.

Mrs Peel *edges towards* **James**.

Mrs Peel   You nip it in the bud right there and then. You take your hand! a rock! a shovel! and you do whatever it takes.

Burns   Any chance a' some breakfast? Been up and out at dawn gettin' this lot.

Mrs Peel   Megan, make Burns some breakfast.

Mrs Peel *starts putting the supplies away.* **Megan** *makes the breakfast. Secret glances are shared between* **James** *and* **Megan** *in the silence. Burns switches the radio on.*

Radio   The government has announced today that more vouchers will be distributed (*Tunes . . .*) Intervals of showers (*Tunes . . .*) Terror and dread fell upon them by the might of your arm. (*Tunes . . .*) And finally may we remind Civilians that there is a strong UV warning tomorrow . . . (*Tunes . . . crazy sermon.*) The Spirit of the Lord God is upon me! –

Burns *switches it off.*

Mrs Peel   Evangelicals, nuttier than a squirrel's fart.

Burns   Spoutin' their horse shit on every network.

James   Same on the streets too.

Burns   Man wants to eat his breakfast and listen to the news.

Mrs Peel   Aint broadcast nothin' true in years.

Turner *and* **Bug** *enter, sweating and soiled from shovelling, they zoom in on the supplies.*

Burns   They don't say the half a' it, I know that.

Turner (*Pulls out the whiskey.*)   Arh yes!

James   Dint even announce that bomb in Leeds.

Everyone turns to **James**. *Beat.*

Turner   What?

Burns   Bomb in Leeds?

Turner   What did you just say?

Bug   Leeds has been bombed!

James   No.

Turner   What did you just say!

Beat.

James (*Quietly.*)   That bomb in Leeds at Security Headquarters. Thought you knew.

Burns   When did this happen?

James   Four . . . five week ago.

Bug   Four, five week ago!

Turner   A' you takin' the piss out a' us?

James   What?

Turner   I said a' you takin' the piss out a' us?

James   No.

Turner   Think you can say bullshit and we'll believe you?

Burns   What happened?

James   A bomb went off –

Turner   We know that!

Burns   Who set it off?

James   Civilians.

Pause.

Bug   Civilians?

Burns   How'd they get inta Headquarters?

James   They blew off the gates.

Turner   How'd they get a bomb?

James   They made it.

Burns   And then what?

James   They sieged the Headquarters.

Beat.

Turner   Sieged?

Burns   How many were they?

James   Eight.

Bug   Eight Civilians sieged a' Headquarters?

Turner   What were the Security doin'!

James (*Shrugs.*)   Sleepin' mostly.

Turner   You tryin' to be funny?

James   It was night, they took 'em by surprise and opened fire.

Bug   What?

James   They had guns, worked in an arms factory.

Turner   And what? We payin' 'em with arms now!

Bug   They'll a smuggled 'em out.

Turner   I know that.

Burns   What was the damage?

James   Communication lines destroyed, women's records burnt, twelve Security dead.

Beat.

Turner   What happened to the eight?

James   Six dead and two executed.

Bug   Why dint we know about this?

Turner   How did you find out?

James   Been told, word a' it spread amongst the Security.

Turner   But nothin' official came through?

James *shakes his head.*

Burns   Playin' down the threat.

Bug   What d'you mean?

Burns   There was always gonna come a day when they'd rise.

Turner (*To* **Bug**.)   Eight dead, dint rise at all.

Burns   It just the beginnin'.

Turner (*To* **Bug**.)   They failed.

Burns   They'll do it again.

Turner (*To* **Burns**.)   It one incident.

Burns   You call that an incident?

Turner   It dint change nothin'.

Bug   Twelve Security dead?

Turner   We soldiers, soldiers die.

Bug   Yeah but overseas.

Burns   War just got closer.

Turner   Ah for fucks sake, eight Civilians!

Bug   You think it gonna lead to that?

Turner (*To* **Bug**.)   Would you shut up!

Burns   It been eight but more will follow.

Turner   They aint never fought back.

Burns   When the elections were cancelled they did.

Turner   And after that day they never done it again.

Pause. **Turner**, **Burns** *and* **Bug** *become very aware of* **Mrs Peel**.

Turner   What did the Civilians a' Leeds do James, after this here *siege*?

James   What d'you mean?

Turner   They dint run on over there and join in?

James   No.

Turner   They dint try again in the weeks that followed?

James (*Shakes his head.*)

Turner   No. They've accepted how things are, same as they accepted how things were gonna be all them years ago, and they aint never done nothin' about it between. (*To* **Bug**.) Bring some a' that whiskey out with us.

Bug *lifts out a bottle.*

James   They were young, the eight.

Turner   Makes no difference.

Bug *and* **Turner** *make to leave.*

James   Think they angry.

Turner   Eight angry teenagers . . . (*Whistles.*) the times we livin' in.

James   Weren't teenagers, been about my age.

Turner   Now I'm really shittin' it.

Burns   It gonna be us they'll come for.

Bug   But we're doin' our job.

Turner   We're here cause the country needed to us be.

Burns   Weren't meant to become this.

Turner   Everythin' we done had to be done.

Bug   What were the government supposed to do?

Turner   We aint here cause a' some ideology.

Burns   Oh I know that, there are no ideas anymore.

Turner   There's the Recovery!

Beat.

Turner   And we're here to ensure that that happens.

Turner *makes to leave.*

Burns   We've got the same debt as a third world country, Turner.

Turner   We are no third world country.

Burns   We could a' prepared for what was to come whilst we still had the money to do so, but no, no, he signed us up to war and debt.

Turner   Don't blame him when it was every other prick in office before him.

Burns   Debt to fight wars that aint even ours.

Turner   Aint ours? The cunts turned the tap off!

Burns   We did not need to join them. And now we'll never be free. We can't pay them back, and they don't want us too. They'd rather have us like this . . . a colony.

Turner   You're gettin' our enemies mixed up.

Burns   They are not our ally.

Turner   And they're not our enemy. Take one look at history and it'll tell you that, yeah, they can be a nasty cunt, but not to us. They always been on our side and when this is over they'll help us with the Recovery.

Burns   There's no Recovery!

Turner   This is England!

Burns   This is not England!

Turner   Then what's your Brian fightin' for if it's not his country?

Burns   My lads not fightin' for his country.

Turner *walks away.*

Burns   He's fightin' for a pipe.

Turner *storms off and* **Bug** *follows.*

Burns   They're fightin' for whatever's left!

Burns *belts back a long drink. Silence.*

Mrs Peel   Like strawberry pie, Burns?

Burns   What?

Mrs Peel   You like strawberry pie?

Burns   Never had it.

Mrs Peel   Megan, fetch me a tin a' strawberries for Burn's pie.

Megan *leaves.* **Mrs Peel** *looks at* **James**, *he leaves.*

Mrs Peel   Ask you a question, Burns?

Burns   Everybody else has.

Mrs Peel   Why a' you in the Security?

Burns   Ask me another.

Mrs Peel   You regret it?

Beat.

Burns   My granddad was a coal miner. Started on the shovel at seventeen. Worked down there till he was fifty five. Lungs packed up when he was fifty nine. He was not a morbid man but over the years he often spoke about his death. Said, I spent most a' my life underground, and when I'm dead, don't put me back down there. (*Turns to* **Mrs Peel**) We buried him.

Mrs Peel   Why?

Burns   Couple a' month before his funeral, he goes to someone else's. My grandma's sat with him in the crematorium. The sad music starts, the doors raised, the coffin gets half way in. My granddad walks out. Grandma leaves when its over, finds him waitin' outside. First thing he says to her, I spent most a' my life down there, and when I'm dead, I'm goin' back down there.

Mrs Peel   Which one does that answer?

Burns   Both.

They share a smile. **Mrs Peel** *walks away.*

Burns   How about whippin' up some cream for my pie Mrs P?

Mrs Peel   I don't do requests or suggestions, Burns. Nor do I do abbreviations. I'm Mrs Peel, always.

Megan *enters with the tin.*

Mrs Peel   Pie'll be ready this evenin'.

Burns *leaves.*

Megan   They never shouted like that.

Mrs Peel   They ballin' all the time.

Megan   Never shouted about them things. Think he said, should a' prepared. You been told what would happen.

Mrs Peel   What a' you sayin' Megan?

Megan *gives the tin to* **Mrs Peel**.

Megan   This pie just for Burns?

Mrs Peel   He havin' the first slice.

Megan   Can I have the second?

Mrs Peel   You can have a' slice too.

Megan   Can I help make it?

Mrs Peel   You wash the slaughter house floor first.

Megan *nods with pursed lips.*

Mrs Peel   You get their uniforms in a tub.

Megan *nods with pursed lips.*

Mrs Peel   You come and tell me then you can roll the pastry.

Megan nods, **Mrs Peel** *turns away.*

James *is about to enter –* **Megan** *shoots her arm up and makes a fist (hold signal) and* **James** *steps back.* **Mrs Peel** *turns to* **Megan,** *who still has her hand in the air.*

Mrs Peel   What a' you doin'?

Megan   Just killed a fly.

Mrs Peel   Open up that hand.

Megan *slowly opens her palm.*

Megan   Thought I killed a fly. (*Looks about.*) It gone.

Mrs Peel *turns away.* **Megan** *looks for* **James** *but he isn't there.*

Megan   Skin a' my hands is cracked and sore.

Mrs Peel   Rub a little butter on 'em.

Megan   Need more than butter.

Mrs Peel   Butter's what you got.

Megan   Put some on my face the other night.

Mrs Peel   You been abusin' that butter?

Megan   Don't want my face to wrinkle.

Mrs Peel   You use it for cracks and sores only.

Megan *sees* **James**'s *head – she crosses her arms across her chest (obstacle.)* **Mrs Peel** *turns to* **Megan,** *who still has her arms across her chest.* **Mrs Peel** *stands staring at* **Megan.** **Megan** *moves her hands about her arms as if they were a lovers.* **Mrs Peel** *looks at* **Megan** *like she's loosing the plot.* **Megan** *finally stops.*

Megan (*Shrugs.*)   Nice to hold yourself sometimes.

Mrs Peel   I'm gonna go and grab hold a' some sheep balls.

Mrs Peel *leaves.* **James** *enters.*

James   She comin' back?

Megan   She gonna' be a while.

James   You sure?

Megan   She got her hands full.

James   Remembered the tactical signals pretty well.

Megan   I did, didn't I.

Beat.

Megan   Have to teach me somethin' else now.

James   Like what?

Megan   Have to think a' somethin'.

Beat.

James   Want a' know some lateral thinkin'?

Megan   Don't have to be from trainin'.

James   Don't know much else.

Megan   Dint sound like that earlier.

James   Burns and Turner done the talkin'.

Megan   You been the one they askin'.

James   Dint have much of an opinion about it.

Megan   You had the facts.

James   Sat there listenin' mostly s'what I done. Reminded me a' when I used to go meetin's with my dad. It been after the Breakdown that. There'd be about fifty a' us, standin' or sittin' in a pokey terrace. I just been a kid, been there listenin'. But the rest a' 'em been talkin' and shoutin' all night. Like I say, been after the Breakdown, could a' made a bonfire out a' their anger. Been that way for about a year, meetin's twice a week. Then he started goin' less, wasn't the only one. He been too tired after his shift or worried that the Security, they'd break up meeting sometimes, would have him down as trouble. He still talked about it all in the evenin's after the news, but he done it with my mum. She always sittin' there quiet. Dint cry no more. When he been promoted to foreman in the factory he stopped goin'. Last meetin' we went to there been a dozen a' us and it finished before the lights went out. (*Shifts.*) This past year I been the one who's breakin' up meetin's . . . they still have 'em in terraces, but they younger who go to 'em . . . aint been any less a' 'em each time we went back . . . I'm talkin' again . . . shouldn't get used to it.

Megan   Aint a bad thing.

James   Good thing. That's why.

Beat.

Megan   When I planted the rhubarb Mrs Peel told me she was gonna make a rhubarb juice with it when it was ready. I never had rhubarb juice before but she told me it's like apple juice but better and I really like apple juice. We started savin' some sugar aside at the beginnin' a' every month for it and after waitin' a whole year it was ready. It was one a' the best things I ever tasted. I had a cup a' it every day for ten days. And then it was gone and I got upset about that. I cried. The next year when the rhubarb was ready Mrs Peel dint make no juice with it. She boiled it up and made me eat it with no sugar for two weeks. That was a long time ago now. Rhubarb's gonna be ready next month and Mrs Peel promised me she gonna make juice with it. When it's gone it's gone. I know that now. I just have to enjoy it whilst its there.

Megan *and* **James** *lean towards one another – a strange rasping noise.*

James   What's that?

Megan (*Softly.*)   Sheep.

Megan *and* **James** *lean further, until they are inches apart – a distressed rasping noise.*

James   Don't sound like sheep.

Megan (*Softly.*)   Mrs Peel's castratin' 'em s'why.

James *jerks backwards.*

James   I gotta go.

James *rushes off, stops.*

James   Tonight?

Megan (*Beams.*)   Tonight.

James *leaves.*

Scene Six

Peak. Sunset.

Turner *and* **Bug** *are sat eating from their tinned cans in silence.*

Bug   I tell yer about that seagull? Don't think I did. When I dropped that deer, eight . . . nine days ago now, anyway, deer's on the ground. I'm makin' my way to it when out a' nowhere a seagull comes down and pecks out the deer's eyeball. If I'd a' been any longer gettin' to it it'd gone straight for its arse hole (*Half laughs.*) . . .

Turner   No fish for 'em.

Beat.

Bug   First thing you said since we been out here.

Turner   Thinkin', s'all.

Bug   Man can think aloud.

Turner   Aint ready in my head yet.

Bug   I say stuff that aint ready all the time.

Turner   I know. S'why I aint.

Beat.

Bug   Thinkin' about what Burns said?

Turner   Nope.

Bug   I been thinkin' about what Burns said.

Beat.

Bug   Pretty fucked, aint it?

Turner   Nope.

Beat.

Bug   How's that.

Turner   I'm sick a' talkin' about. Sick a' thinkin' about it. Don't even matter to me anymore. Recovery or no Recovery, it aint gonna make no difference to me and what I'm gonna do. I served my country. I done my duty. I aint doin' it . . . I aint.

Bug   What?

Turner   Fuck 'em. Fuck 'em all.

Bug   What a' you talkin' about?

Turner   I'm gonna find myself an abandoned farm. Fix it up. And stay the fuck there.

(*Beat.*)

Could be there too if yer wanted.

(*Beat.*)

Turner   World already got smaller, and it can get even smaller for me. It can get as small as a farm and a couple a' acres a' land. It can empty itself a' everybody till there's just me and you left. It can burn itself to the ground around us.

Beat.

Turner   Man can't be alone. (*Glances at* **Bug**.) I know what time a' day it is with you and . . . you do me. Way I see it, we'd get along fine anywhere's.

Beat.

Turner   Anyway, that's what I'm gonna do.

Pause.

Turner   What you gone quiet for!

Bug   I'm just listenin'.

Turner   Told you I dint want a' say nothin'!

Turner *stands.*

Turner   Said it wrong cause you're fuckin' quizzin' me.

Bug   I aint quizzin' you.

Turner   You're fuckin' quizzin' me all the fuckin' time.

Bug   Ah, fuck this.

Turner   Yeah, fuck you.

Bug *walks away. Both men stand opposite, backs turned. Pause.*

Bug   Prick.

Turner   Wanker.

Bug   Cock.

Turner   Cock sucker.

Bug   Cunt.

Turner   Cunty bollocks.

Bug   Spunk ball.

Turner   Spunk ball?

Bug   Spunk ball.

Turner   Inventive.

They take out their flasks, swig one back.

Bug   Reddest sky I seen tonight.

Turner   Reckon it's gonna rain?

Bug   Can't never tell.

Turner *and* **Bug** *become alert – the clack and ricochet of stag's antlers.*

Bug   Stags.

Turner *looks away, but* **Bug** *continues to stare out.*

Turner   Lucky bastards.

Bug   They aint ruttin'.

Turner   Next life I'm comin' back as a stag.

Bug   They chargin' forwards, they fightin'.

Turner   Fuck me they even get foreplay.

Turner *sits down by the fire.*

Bug   What you been sayin' earlier.

Turner   Forget about that.

Bug   Makes sense to me. Never thought about it but soon as you said it, had it all figured in my head. I even seen the place, Turn. Everythin' just fell inta place . . . Except for one thing.

Turner   What?

Bug   How we gonna get it?

Turner   Need to think it over.

Bug   You said it'd be an abandoned farm?

Turner *doesn't answer, he drinks from his flask.*

Bug   Means it'd be outside a' the restrictions.

Turner   They all been emptied years before that.

Bug   Don't matter if it were before or after.

Turner *stands, shifts about agitated.*

Turner   Restrictions don't apply to us.

Bug   They would if we weren't in the Security no more.

Turner *becomes still.*

Turner   Restrictions aint gonna be forever. (*Turns to* **Bug**.) Gotta lift 'em some time.

Bug *nods and they look away from each other.*

Bug   Where we settin' up for the night?

Turner   Castleton.

Turner *picks up his rifle*

Bug   Had this thing happen there.

Turner   What thing?

Bug   Felt somethin' watchin' me.

Turner   What'd you mean?

Bug   Even though I was sleepin', I knew it was there.

Turner *walks off.*

Turner (*Calls back.*)   I've dreamt a pussy and woke up fuckin' tastin' it.

Bug   Wasn't a dream.

Turner *has left.* **Bug** *picks up his rifle and turns to leave. He stands motionless as he sees the figure of a man in the distance. The man's head is lowered and he wears a crown made of stag's antlers, smeared in blood. The man drops to his knees. A wind rises.*

Scene Seven

Slaughter room. Morning. The wind howls.

A deer bound by its back legs hangs down from an iron grip. The bucket directly below it collects the blood as it bleeds out. **Megan** *is holding the knife at the deer,* **Mrs Peel** *stands behind her.*

Mrs Peel   Start at her crotch and take it all the way to her breast.

Megan *draws the line with the blade.*

Mrs Peel   Don't show her all a' yer blade, just the tip, give enough to get under her hide.

Megan *brings the blade back.*

Mrs Peel   You do the same thing again but this time you givin' it more, give her a half inch, that'll open her up. Don't get carried away, cause if you do, you gonna be in her stomach.

Burns *enters.*

Burns   Nearly got killed makin' my way here.

Mrs Peel (*To* **Megan**.)   Start steelin' the blade.

Burns   Some loose tiles fell not more than a foot away from me.

Mrs Peel   Not seen a wind like this before, couple a' fence posts heaved themselves clean out a' the soil durin' the night.

Mrs Peel *sees that* **Burns** *has been drinking.*

Mrs Peel   Need somethin' Burns?

Burns   Listened to the radio this mornin'?

Mrs Peel   We graftin' from since six nowadays.

Burns   Kings dead.

Megan *stops steeling the blade.*

Burns   Died over there last night. They've lost the strong hold. They aint bringin' anyone back.

Mrs Peel *watches* **Burns** *drink from his flask.*

Burns   Yer gonna have two less mouths to feed as a' tomorrow.

Mrs Peel   Who been drafted?

Burns   Bug and James.

Mrs Peel   They bein' replaced?

Burns   No one to replace 'em. They sendin' thousands to Venezuela. It just gonna be me and Turner out here.

The wind shrieks.

Burns   Damn wind.

Mrs Peel   Somethin' cooler is settin' in.

Burns   You reckon its here to stay?

Mrs Peel   I do.

Beat.

Mrs Peel   Anythin' else?

Burns   Put a half bottle a' whiskey under the sink yesterday.

Mrs Peel   Already seen it.

Burns   You don't miss a trick, Mrs Peel.

Mrs Peel   I got twenty twenty vision, Burns.

Turner *storms in followed by* **Bug**.

Turner   We need to talk!

Burns   No point talkin' to me about it.

Bug   Come on, Turn.

Turner   Why aint I goin'?

Burns   I don't decide who goes and who stays.

Turner   But you can do somethin' about it.

Bug   It been decided, Turn.

Turner   He aint goin' without me.

Burns   Nothin' I can do about it.

Turner   This is bullshit.

Burns   Turner! I wouldn't hesitate in sendin' you instead that boy if I could.

Turner   I want to go!

Bug   It aint up to him.

Turner   I'm leavin' tomorrow.

Bug   You can't do that.

Turner   I'm takin' James's place.

Bug   They won't allow it.

Turner   What the fucks he gonna do out there? He don't know shit. He aint gonna last a week.

Bug   You know the drill, Turn.

Turner   Would you shut up.

Bug   Ah fuck this.

Turner   Yeah fuck you.

Megan (*From the gut.*)   Stop!

Everyone turns to **Megan**. *Pause.*

Megan (*Trembling.*)   I got a deer to skin.

James *enters,* **Megan** *turns away.*

Mrs Peel   What d'you want?

James   Hares a' eatin' tops a' your courgettes.

Mrs Peel   What did I tell you! Don't just stand there –

James   There's too many a' 'em.

Mrs Peel (*Gravely.*)   How many?

James   Five.

Mrs Peel *draws her blade and breath.*

Mrs Peel   Megan, get yourself a shovel.

Mrs Peel *rushes off.*

Mrs Peel   We're bein' overun!

Megan *leaves without looking at* **James**. **Burns** *looks at* **Turner** *and* **Bug**.

Burns   Say we go finish the last a' that pie?

Burns *and* **James** *leave.*

Bug   Don't see why you're pissed at me.

Beat.

Bug   Aint nothin' I can do about it, Turn.

Turner   Its bullshit!

Bug   It just the way it goes. You know that.

Turner   Fuckin' sick a' it, s'what I know.

Bug   Aint like I'm not comin' back here.

Turner   When! A year? Two? Three –

Bug   Shit I don't know.

Turner   I do! I know that we got plans. I know that we can see them plans through. This. This here situation, don't ruin them plans if we don't let it. What it does is bring them plans closer. We been talkin' about doin' this thing later, fuck it, we do it now. We do it tonight. We camp out. We don't come back here.

Pause.

Bug   You talkin' about bein' an Illegal, Turn.

Turner   We aint gonna be Illegals.

Bug   S'what you sayin'.

Turner   S'fuckin' word that don't mean shit for us.

Bug   S'word that gets us struck off the register.

Turner   We don't need to be on it.

Bug   What a' you talkin' about?

Turner   We'd be self sufficient. We wouldn't need any a' their tinned hand outs. We'd be on our own and botherin' nobody. We wouldn't be livin' in a squalor terrace. We'd find a place in the middle a' nowhere, we know the drill Bug. We know where Security go and don't go –

Bug   We are Security!

Turner   I know what we are. And I know what we could be.

Beat.

Bug   I aint doin' it till we can do it right. I couldn't be alright with what I done over these years if I thought that given the chance I'd do same as them.

Turner   I aint the same as them!

Bug   I dint say that –

Turner   I fought in war after war –

Bug   I never said you dint.

Turner   You never said nothin'.

Turner *leaves.*

Scene Eight

Stables. Evening. Violent rain.

James *waits.* **Megan** *enters.*

James   Dint know if you were gonna come.

Megan   Just passin' by.

James   Been waitin here all night.

Megan   Washed my hair.

James   Haven't had a chance –

Megan   Don't want to talk about it.

Pause.

Megan   Mince hasn't been eatin'.

Beat.

James   Didn't know that.

Megan   Two days now.

James   Not like him.

Beat.

Megan   Chickens haven't laid eggs.

James   Had an egg this morning.

Megan   You had an old egg.

Beat.

James   Megan –

Megan   Don't want to talk about it.

Pause.

Megan   Dropped a plate this afternoon.

Beat.

James   It break?

Megan   Million pieces.

James   Megan stop –

Megan   Don't want to talk about it.

Beat.

Megan   Beans a' spoilt.

Beat.

Megan   A tree fell.

Beat.

Megan   Barn door's smashed.

Beat.

Megan   Cow's dead.

Beat.

Megan (*Cries.*)   Don't want to cry about it.

James *goes towards her but she steps back.*

Megan   Don't want to be left behind.

James   Don't want to leave.

Megan   Don't want to be alone.

James   I'm coming back.

James *moves closer to her.*

Megan   Don't want to wait.

James   Ssshh.

Megan   Don't want to want.

James   Ssshh.

Megan   Don't want to want you.

Beat.

Megan   Want you.

James   Want you too.

Megan   Want you to love me.

James   Already do.

Beat.

James   Love you.

Pause.

Megan   Love you.

Beat.

James   I love you.

Beat.

Megan (*Smiles.*)   I love you.

James (*Smiles.*)   I love you.

Megan (*Smiles.*)   I love you.

James (*Laughs.*)   I love you!

Megan (*Laughs.*)   I love you!

James (*Shouts.*)   I love you!

Megan   Ssshh. Want you to make love to me.

Blackout.

Act Two

Scene One

Kitchen. Noon. Violent rain.

Mrs Peel *and* **Megan** *are stacking and checking crates of vegetables.* **Burns** *enters jauntily, carrying a rifle and wet from rain.*

Burns   I just hung you up a fine young hind.

Mrs Peel   That don't mean pig pee to me right now Burns.

Burns *puts the rifle down, notices the crates.*

Mrs Peel   Barn roof fixin' up s'what I need.

Burns   It comin' in bad?

Mrs Peel   I've stopped counting how much I've lost to fungus.

Burns   Nothin' I can do about it in this rain.

Mrs Peel   He's got me by the balls this time.

Burns   Soon as it stops I'll get up there, see to it.

Mrs Peel   Should a' been seen to before now.

Burns   I done some a' it.

Mrs Peel   That been six week ago.

Burns   Few days work and it'll be finished. Never seen so many hares about. Must a' been a spike in 'em, bought back two a' them as well. Almost missed the hind, was takin' a piss when I seen it and just as I'm at the trigger somethin' must a' spooked it cause it bolted.

Mrs Peel (*Lowers her gaze.*)   Dint finish that job neither.

Burns *zips up his fly.* **Turner** *enters, wet and sulky.*

Turner   I aint campin' up the grit stone no more. Aint had a piss in two days, case I got fast there on the spot. Aint had a wash and I'm salty as a wet dog. Fuckin' stupid-cuntin' tent caved in on me twice. I had to wallop my boots inta that bastard horse's lungs to get it to budge. And I been on a saddle way to fuckin' hell and back. I aint campin' up the grit stone no more!

Beat.

Turner   Cup a' tea'd be nice.

Mrs Peel *puts the tea on.*

Burns   I was gonna ask for that nice hare and onion stew you made for us one time?

Mrs Peel   Aint makin' that again, makes you fart.

Burns   Only . . . Bug's gettin' back here today.

Mrs Peel   I definitely aint makin' no stew.

Megan *is devastated.*

Turner   You dint tell me that!

Burns   You just got in.

Turner   When's he comin'?

Burns   Tonight.

Turner   Shit. We aint ready. we done nothin' for him.

Burns   Be nice to make him that stew.

Mrs Peel   He gonna get what he get.

Megan   This must be a good sign.

Turner   He aint gonna want no stew.

Megan   Must mean they gonna send more back.

Turner   He gonna want lamb.

Mrs Peel   He aint getting' it.

Megan   They say that, Burns?

Turner   We gotta get one a' them lambs on a spit.

Mrs Peel   I need them sheep for milk.

Turner   You don't need all a' 'em.

Mrs Peel   Sheep only got two teats, I need every teat I got!

Turner   I knowed he gonna come back. How the fuck he swing that?

Stands and raises his flask.

To that jammy fuckin' bastard.

Burns   To bringin' 'em home.

Megan *has finally got her answer.*

Megan   To bringin' 'em home.

Chink – they belt one back. **Megan** *and* **Turner** *are up and about the kitchen.*

Turner   We'll camp out early tonight.

Megan   We should all celebrate here.

Burns   don't go throwin' that bag out, can get another cup out a' that.

Mrs Peel (*Dumps the tea bag.*)   I know how to make a cup a' tea.

Turner   Take some steaks out with us.

Megan   You could both stay here.

Burns   Now why'd you do that?

Mrs Peel   I made three cups out a' it.

Turner   We got some sides a' deer.

Megan   That way we could all hear about it.

Burns   I know, I was watchin'.

Mrs Peel   That bag had nothin' in it left to give.

Turner   We aint got enough whisky!

Burns   I think it has a little more life in it yet.

Mrs Peel   One bag can make up to three cups.

Burns   Looks like yer got yourself a challenge there, Mrs Peel, cause I can make four.

Mrs Peel   I can make ten if you want 'em weak as cat piss!

Burns   I can make four cups, strong as they come, with one bag.

Mrs Peel   You're a bare-faced liar, Burns.

Burns   (*Staring at her.*) Turner, get me a tea bag and four cups.

Mrs Peel   (*Staring at him.*) Make that two bags and seven cups.

Beat. Everyone turns to **Turner**.

Turner (*Disbelief.*)   What?

Turner *does it.*

Burns   Who's judgin'?

Mrs Peel   You choose.

Burns   Which one of youse knows a good cuppa?

Megan *shoots her hand into the air.*

Burns   Alright, Megan it is. Second thing. What's at stake here?

Mrs Peel   What d'you mean?

Burns   We're doin' prizes.

Mrs Peel   Prizes?

Megan   Prizes!

Mrs Peel   Alright. You first.

Burns   I'd like to have a dance.

Beat.

Mrs Peel   What d'you mean?

Burns   I'd like to dance.

Mrs Peel (*Indifferent.*)   Alright.

Burns   You and me.

Turner   What?

Mrs Peel   I aint dancin'.

Burns   Man can't dance alone.

Mrs Peel   I aint dancin' with you, Burns.

Megan   I will!

Burns   Thought you was gonna' win?

Beat.

Mrs Peel   Alright. Stakes it is. I want a' go out on them moors with yer and get a deer.

Burns   Alright.

Turner   What?

Burns (*To* **Megan**.)   Ready?

Megan *begins the tasting, starting with* **Mrs Peel**'s *three cups.*

Megan   They all good.

Mrs Peel *sniffs with pride and* **Megan** *moves on to* **Burns**'s *cups.*
Megan *maximizes her time as the centre of attention – she sips, slurps, ponders and gurgles.*

Megan   They all good!

Mrs Peel   You win.

Turner *pats* **Burns** *on the back,* **Megan** *claps,* **Mrs Peel** *smiles.*
Bug *enters, his left arm is now a stump.*

Turner   You're early.

Bug *drops his bag down.*

Turner   Nothin's ready.

Bug   S'alright.

Megan *looks as if she might burst into tears, she leaves.*

Burns (*Shakes his hand.*)   Good to have yer back.

Bug   Good to be back.

Turner   Where the fuck you been?

Turner *slings his arms around* **Bug**, *they wrestle and laugh.* **Mrs Peel** *leaves.*

Turner   Fuckin' leavin' me.

Burns   Let's have a drink.

They belt one back.

Turner (*Nods to the stump.*)   So, what happened there then?

Bug   Lost it.

Turner   It giver yer any trouble?

Bug   Can hurt. Just adaptin' to it.

Turner   Least you can still pull your prick.

Burns   How's Brian?

Bug   We were nowhere near his regiment.

Burns   What? But you were south.

Bug   Couldn't get no word to him.

Turner   How's James?

Burns   You get my letter to him?

Bug   I'm sorry, Burns.

Turner   He doin' us proud?

Burns   A they bringin' any a' 'em back?

Bug   There are soldiers . . . there are soldiers . . .

Beat. **Burns** *sits down.*

Turner   Want somethin' to eat?

Bug   I'm alright with this.

Turner   What'd they drink over there?

Bug   Rum.

Turner   S'alright.

Bug   Yeah. Prefer whiskey.

Turner   We aint got much a' it.

Bug   They shippin' less over?

Turner   Halved our supplies, s'only thing we get short a'.
Way we set up here now, we eatin' none a' that tinned shit.
It gonna be steak and taters we puttin' on the fire tonight.
Times we back here we getting' meat and two veg, stews
with mash . . . all kinds a' shit. And then there's breakfast.
Full on fried breakfast!

Bug   Sounds good. So what's been goin' on?

Turner   Jack shit been happenin' out here.

Bug   Not many Illegals?

Turner   We aint been gettin' many. Its impossible to do the
job, just the two a' us out there. (*Chinks Bug's flask.*) But
that's all set to change now eh?

Bug   What about outside?

Turner (*Shrugs.*)   Government set up a lottery for them that
want kids.

Bug   They lifted the ban?

Turner   S'lottery, Bug.

Bug   Right.

Turner   One in ten thousand. How long it take to get back?

Bug   What about China?

Turner (*Shrugs.*)   What about it?

Bug   Allies declared war two week ago.

Turner   Aint affectin' us, none a' our troops a' bein' deployed.

Bug   It a different war they startin' over there.

Turner   How long it take to get back?

Bug   Near on three days.

Turner   Shit.

Bug   Yeah. Tried to get a few winks on the train up there.

Turner   Too worried for that, I bet.

Bug   Well . . . I'm gonna go crash for a couple a' hours.

Turner   Now?

Bug *nods.*

Turner   You just got here.

Bug   I'm tired, Turn.

Turner   Alright.

Bug goes back to his bag.

Bug   Bought you a piece a' kit back.

Turner   Arh, yes! It some a' their kit?

Bug   Yeah.

Turner   Vest? Pair a' eyes?

Bug   Aint nothin' like that. It a radio.

Bug *gives the radio to* **Burns**.

Burns (*Nods.*)   Good to have yer back.

Turner   I'll come and get yer in a couple a' hours.

Bug *nods and leaves.*

Turner   Why the fuck dint you tell me he'd got a stump?

Burns   I dint know.

Turner   Must a' looked like a right cunt, dint know what to say.

Burns   Coulda fooled me, pullin' his prick.

Turner   I can't treat him like he's disabled. It's Bug, same old, arm or no arm. And anyway, that's what yer supposed to do . . . acknowledge it.

Beat.

Can you ride a horse with a stump?

Burns *shrugs, drinks.*

Burns   Now we know how come he's back.

Turner   Yeah.

Burns   Never seen him like that.

Turner   Tired, s'all.

Burns   More than that.

Turner   Couple a' hours sleep he'll be right.

Burns   Seen it in his eyes.

Burns *leaves with the radio.*

Turner   He gonna be fine.

Scene Two

Stables. Evening.

Megan *is sat, she has been crying.* **Turner** *enters stealthy.*

Megan (*Spins round.*)   You scared me!

Turner   Whooah. You been cryin'?

Megan   No.

Turner   Looks to me like you have.

Megan   Haven't.

Turner (*Offers her a fag.*)   Fag? You sure?

Megan   Don't smoke.

Turner   Since when?

Megan   Never liked 'em much.

Turner   Used to smoke a lot a' mine to say you din't like 'em.

Beat.

Turner   Want a' talk about it?

Megan   Nothin' a' talk about.

Turner   Might help if you did. I'll take a guess. You seen what happened to Bug and you worried about James.

Megan   Why would I be worried about him?

Turner   I seen him headin' over here at night, Megan. And I knowed you in here too. I dint say nothin' to you about it. Just accepted it I guess. Don't mean that I stopped . . . shit, you know . . . carin' about you.

Megan *looks at* **Turner**.

Turner   S'how you holdin' up?

Megan   Miss him. Miss him a lot.

Turner   Yeah. I bet he's missin' you too. Who wouldn't? You're quite a girl Megan. I'll tell you somethin' from experience. When a man's been with you it's pretty hard to come back from that. Yeah. You really set the standard for me. Raised the bar. And in all sorts a' ways, not just . . . (*Laughs with embarrassment.*) You know. Shit. I aint no good at this. I just wanted to see you were alright. I'm gonna' go. Leave you to it.

Turner *walks away.*

Megan   Stay.

Turner   Well, alright.

Megan   We could talk.

Turner   I'd like that.

Beat.

Megan   Bird flew inta the kitchen window yesterday.

Turner   Yeah?

Megan   I was right there in front a' it washin' the dishes when it hit the glass. Made a big thuddin' sound, scared me. Then it flew off. But it left somethin' behind. A white powder in the shape a' it wings. Like a ghost a' it. I been lookin' at that all day and no one seen it, not even Mrs Peel. I dint tell her, case she rubbed it away.

Turner   I'll have to take a look at that.

Megan   Won't be there no more cause a' the rain.

Turner   Some things just don't last long enough, do they?

Beat.

Megan   Never knowed you cared about me.

Turner   I'm no good at sayin' stuff like that.

Megan   That mean you'd look out for me?

Turner   I done it before, remember.

Beat.

You were gonna be sent away.

Megan   I know

Turner   Don't seem like it.

Megan   You told me. But it different now.

Turner   It sure is. S'like you been avoidin' me.

Megan   You'd help me if . . . if I needed it?

Turner   You know I would.

Megan   James would too.

Turner   But he aint here.

Megan   He gonna come back. Just don't know when.

Turner *takes out his flask politely offers* **Megan** *a drink.*

Megan   I shouldn't.

Turner   Why?

Megan   It too early for that.

Turner   Have a slug anyway, for old time's sake.

Megan *drinks; spills some down her chin.*

Turner   Looks like you forgotten how to handle your drink.

They both laugh; she gives him back the flask.

Turner   Come on, you can do better than that.

Megan *shakes her head.* **Turner** *insists.* **Megan** *has another drink.*

Turner   S'like old times. We did have us some good times together. You remember that time when you, me and Bug been up all night drinkin'? You were drinkin' like a fish, couldn't get enough a' the stuff.

Megan   I got work to do now.

Turner   Laughin' and smilin' you were.

Megan *tries to pass but* **Turner** *blocks her way.*

Turner   You do have a lovely smile. Really lights up a room, lights up . . . (*Smiles.*) Anyway, so there we all are with an empty bottle on the table between us. Not a drop left. And you . . . (*Laughs.*)

Megan   Don't!

Turner   You took hold a' the bottle.

Megan   Please don't.

Turner   And let us both have a go. Didn't you? What's this . . . tears? No, no, you don't understand. I dint tell James about it. I wouldn't do that. I wouldn't spoil what you got goin' there. Cause, it would. Wouldn't it? I mean, if he knew that what sweet Megan here likes (*shakes his head and laughs to himself.*) and I mean really likes is bein' fucked dirty. He would feel insecure about that. Cause he didn't fuck you like that. Did he? (*Sympathetically.*) I dint think so.

Megan   Leave me alone.

Turner   I wish I could, but when you look at me with those sad eyes a' yours, s'like lookin' at a deer before I slam it down to the ground. Gets me hard.

Turner *takes off his jacket,* **Megan** *edges backwards.*

Turner   See, all's I want is to throw you a nice, hard fuck. Yeah, that's right. (*Edges forwards.*) All's I want is to take that nice long hair a' yours and use it like a pair a' reigns. (*Grabs* **Megan**'s *hair.*) Alls I want is to saddle up and –

The horses whinny. **Burns** *enters.*

Burns   What's goin' on here!

Turner *releases* **Megan**.

Turner   Nothin'.

Burns   I don't give a flyin' fuck that you out here in the wilderness, you wanna' shove that dick a' yours in somethin' I suggest you start takin' a likin' to livestock. That understood?

Turner *nods.* **Burns** *steps aside.* **Turner** *leaves.*

Burns   He bother you again, you come to me about it.

Burns *makes to leave.*

Megan   It a good sign, Bug comin' back?

Burns   You seen his arm.

Megan   He came back alive.

Burns   They don't bring the dead back.

Beat.

Burns   Been waitin' three years for my boy to come back.
You can't keep waitin'.

Burns *leaves.* **Megan** *drops to her knees and cries. The horses
whinny.* **James**, *dressed in civvies, enters.* **Megan** *slowly stands to
her feet and looks at* **James** *for a few seconds. She smiles and he
smiles back at her. She laughs and he laughs. She slowly walks
towards him, the distant sound of gunfire and explosions are heard,
until they are stood opposite one another.*

James   It a gift.

James *edges backwards away from* **Megan** *as the sound of gunfire
and explosions become louder and call him back, until he finally
disappears.*

Scene Three

Peak. Late afternoon. **Bug** *and* **Turner** *are sat quietly drinking.*

Bug   Missed this quiet.

Turner   Like it too, but shit I had enough a' it these past
months.

Bug   Been on your own out here?

Turner   Pretty much. wind, hoof beats . . . caw of a bird,
that been it for me.

Bug   My ears a' still ringing.

Turner   Get laid much.

Bug   Wasn't like that.

Turner (*Shakes his flask.*)   Shit, this aint gonna last us two days.

Bug   Way you been going at it, it aint gonna get us to tonight.

Turner   We need to take this situation in hand.

Bug   What d'you mean?

Turner   Taters make vodka, right?

Bug   Yeah, but, you need somethin' else too.

Turner   What?

Bug   Alcohol I guess.

Turner *and* **Bug** *laugh a little.*

Turner   S'what I missed the most, talkin' shit to somebody. There been times out here when the drag of a cloud been the biggest event a' my day. don't know how I've done it. (*Drinks.*) But it given me the time to figure a' few things, like I said was gonna . . . about that place a' ours. Not that cock-eyed-bullshit I been spoutin' before you left. (*Half laughs.*) The shit I been spewin'. I can be a crazy bastard sometimes, I know that. But you should a' just laid one on me. Had it a' been the other way round I'd a done it to you. I don't mean that. It'll be when it'll be. But. Just how you seen it that first time I told it, I seen it too.

Bug   Turn . . .

Turner   I aint shittin' you. There been times up on that saddle, when I seen it right there on the horizon. Perched on its own, nothin' but weather around it. I'd keep on its trail, laughin' at myself some, knowin' it aint there . . . but the horse'd pick it up a little, like it felt the pull a' it too. It'd still be some fifty mile a' so ahead a' me, when I'd start to see them stones it made up a', solid granite, every one a' 'em . . . pokey windows that don't let much light in. After a while I'd throw my eyeline away and when I looked back it wouldn't be there no more . . . but soon as the sun dropped, I'd see an orange glut a' flame from the fireplace. There'd be steak and taters on it, pile a' cards at the ready . . .

Beat.

Turner   S'gonna be lot a' fuckin' work too. Aint gonna be how I'm tellin' it now when we get hold a' it. But way I see it every inch a' fencin' we put up, every plank a' wood we sand, every blister on our backs, be worth it cause it's for us. Our own fuckin' thing.

Beat.

Bug   Been thinkin' I'd a' liked to a' been married again.

Turner (*Laughs.*)   Married?

Bug   Yeah.

Turner (*Stops laughing.*)   You never told me you been married.

Bug   Me and her been eighteen, had ourselves the biggest weddin'. Three white limo's, nine bridesmaids, three page boys, hundred and forty eight guests, seven tier wedding cake, and a mountain a' profiteroles with a six foot chocolate fountain for them that dint like icin' or dried fruit. She left me after three months to start up with the weddin' photographer. He said he could get her modellin' career goin' . . . We'd a' had a baby we'd a' been alright.

Turner   Best thing you did gettin' rid a' her.

Bug   We been arguin' most a the time, dint laugh twice.

Turner   That's it, birds aren't funny.

Bug   Some birds a' funny.

Turner   Name one bird we know who's funny?

Bug   We don't any birds . . . Mrs Peel got a sense a' humour.

Turner   She got a crusty fanny as well. Dint think about the wives.

Bug   Just sayin' it's somethin' I'd a' liked to a done before now.

Beat.

Bug   Shouldn't think about gettin' that place, Turn.

Turner   Why's that?

Bug   Can't see it no more.

Turner   Yeah? Well I can.

Bug   Don't see us here much longer.

Turner   What a' you talkin' about?

Bug   Need all the men they got.

Turner   Need men back here too.

Bug   Somethin's gotta give.

Turner   Security's weak as it is.

Bug   Bulk a' the army aint enough.

Turner   Fuck it I'll go and come back.

Bug   There aint no comin' back.

Turner   What a' you fuckin' sayin'?

Bug   They aint comin' back.

Turner   You fuckin' did.

Bug   Set the grenade off myself.

Pause.

Turner   Had our backs to the wall plenty a' times.

Bug   Aint like what it been before.

Turner   I know what it's fuckin' like.

Bug   No you don't.

Turner   I fuckin' do!

Bug   There aint no talkin' to you sometimes.

Turner   Not when you're talkin' shit.

Bug   You don't wanna' hear it.

Turner   There aint nothin' you can tell me.

Turner *turns around.* **Bug** *stays as he is.*

Turner   You're just pissed about your arm.

Bug   You dint hear what I said.

Turner   I fuckin' heard yer. I don't believe yer.

Turner *is striding aimlessly behind* **Bug**.

Turner   You . . . you couldn't a' done that. You hear! You
dint do that . . . leave me waitin' out here . . . weren't gonna
do that . . . couldn't a' left me out here . . . You wanna drop
me? S'that what you fuckin' want? Need to take that stump
out on someone? Go ahead. I can take it. Come on. Lay one
on me. Fuckin' turn around. Fuckin' come on and get it.
(*Draws back a blow.*) I'll fuck you –

A fighter jet screeches overhead. **Turner** *hits the ground,* **Bug**
doesn't react.

Turner   Shit! Shit shit shit did you hear that? (*Laughs.*) We
got jets. (*On his knees.*) We . . . we got jets.(*On his feet.*) We got
jets in the sky! Woo-Hoo!

Bug   Aint ours.

Beat.

Turner   What?

Bug   Jets, aint ours.

Turner   What d'you mean?

Bug   Our allies set up an airbase outside a' Sheffield.

Turner   What a' they doin' here?

Bug   Firin' misiles.

Turner Where to?

Bug China. Turn, they been –

Turner Still, good to see somethin' up there.

Turner *stares at* **Bug** *defiantly. Pause.* **Bug** *walks away.*

Bug Goin' back to the outpost tomorrow.

Turner We out here for two days.

Another fighter jet screeches overhead. Turner runs after it, making whooping noises.

Scene Four

Plot of land. Sunset.

Mrs Peel *is harvesting potatoes from the earth.* **Burns** *enters, he has been drinking heavily but wears it well. He stands at a distance to her looking out.*

Burns Quite a sunset.

Beat.

Burns More orange than usual. Don't yer think?

Mrs Peel Aint lookin' at it.

Burns Late in the day to be doin' that.

Burns *edges closer to* **Mrs Peel**.

Burns That was a fine dinner.

Mrs Peel Not keen on snails.

Burns Don't like the taste or the look a' 'em?

Mrs Peel Just don't fancy 'em after lookin' at 'em shit all day.

Burns I been meanin' to ask what yer put with 'em?

Mrs Peel Garlic and sage. Same as I do everythin'.

Burns   Used to do a bit a' cookin' myself.

Mrs Peel   Let me know if you should get the urge again.

Burns   I wouldn't be able to do what you do.

Mrs Peel   I'm out a' whiskey.

Burns   Got some here.

Burns *gives his flask to* **Mrs Peel**.

Burns   I'm getting' supplies in the mornin'.

Mrs Peel *gives the flask back.*

Burns   Put you a bottle under the sink.

Mrs Peel *doesn't acknowledge the bottle; continues working.*

Burns   What a' you cookin' for dinner tomorrow?

Mrs Peel   Snails.

Burns   Again?

Mrs Peel   Had to put some a' em aside. They weren't shittin'.

Burns   Constipated snails?

Mrs Peel   And mashed tater.

Burns   Been thinkin' about makin' some changes around here.

Mrs Peel   What kind a' changes?

Burns   Not now.

Mrs Peel *stands.*

Mrs Peel   What kind a changes?

Burns   A greenhouse.

The potato falls away from **Mrs Peel**'*s hand.*

Burns   Build a greenhouse so as we can get more fruit. Fix the roofin' a' the stables. Make a stone oven for outside.

Take some cuttin's and plant some flowers. Get some beehives. Four, five beehives for honey and . . . what's that other stuff called yer get from 'em?

Mrs Peel   Royal jelly.

Burns   Yeah, royal jelly. What d'yer say?

Mrs Peel (*Becomes* **Mrs Peel**.)   More work. But. Alright.

Beat.

Burns   How come in all this time I never known your first name?

Mrs Peel   Cause I never told yer, Burns.

Burns   It's Keith . . . Keith. Is it out a' respect for a Mr Peel?

Mrs Peel   Are you drunk!

Burns   No.

Mrs Peel (*Crouches down.*)   Then stop talkin' shit.

Mrs Peel *shoves potatoes into the sack,* **Burns** *crouches down before her.*

Burns (*Takes the sack.*)   Why ruin what we got here?

Mrs Peel (*Grabs the sack back.*)   We aint got nothin'.

Burns   But we could have.

Burns *swoops* **Mrs Peel** *onto her back and arches over her like a dog.*

Mrs Peel   Bleedin' 'ell fire and Jack!

Burns   Mrs Peel you got enough balls for ten men, can drink any man under the table, give a man as good as yer get, swear like a trooper, work harder than most a' the men I know. And yet! You've got the bosom of a Goddess. (*Bends forwards.*) The carriage of an eagle. And I bet your packin' as much heat in that cave a' yours as the earth's core. (*Bends forwards.*) That bein' with you would be a *hot* and *molten* –

Mrs Peel *slaps* **Burns**'*s face.*

Burns (*Strokes his cheek.*)   How about you and me take a moonlight swim?

Mrs Peel   I could choke you.

Mrs Peel *bolts to her feet and* **Burns** *chases after her.*

Mrs Peel   You wanna' keep that dead squid a' yours away from me!

Burns   I can assure you it's *alive*!

Mrs Peel *grabs a shovel and threatens to clobber* **Burns** *with it.*

Mrs Peel   It won't be if you come any closer.

Burns   Why don't you and me step inside and get to it?

Mrs Peel   I'd rather be under a rabid dog.

Burns   How about we just drop the lip on?

Mrs Peel   I'd rather be sat on the shitter with diarrhoea and toothache.

Burns   We could have ourselves a cuddle?

Mrs Peel   I'd rather . . . I got a tough enough life as it is without stavin' off the advances of a sex maniac! (*From the gut.*) Now step away!

Burns *does.*

Mrs Peel   I don't know who you think you're playin' with.

Burns   I aint playin'.

Mrs Peel *walks away.*

Burns   I'm sweet on you!

Beat.

Burns   How about you and me go get your deer?

Mrs Peel *stops.*

Burns   Tomorrow?

Beat.

Burns   That a date?

Beat.

Mrs Peel   I guess.

Mrs Peel *leaves.*

Scene Five

Kitchen. Morning.

Megan *is folding a pile of washed and dried clothes and sheets.*
Bug *enters.*

Bug   I been needin' to talk to you too.

Megan   Me?

Beat.

Megan   Why?

Beat. **Megan** *sees it in* **Bug**'*s eyes. She grabs a sheet from the pile.*

Megan   Give me a hand foldin' these sheets?

Bug *looks at his stump.*

Megan   We'll just fold it best we can.

Bug   Can we sit down?

Megan   They so big we got a' stand and do it.

Megan *gives some of the sheet to* **Bug** *to hold on to.*

Megan   You keep hold a' this here.

Bug   I need to tell you somethin'.

Megan *steps away from* **Bug**.

Megan   I can hear you from here.

Megan *takes the corners and opens the stained sheet out.*

Megan   Don't know how these stains got here.

Megan *halves the width of the sheet.*

Bug   Its James.

Megan *halves the width of the sheet again.*

Megan   I think it Burns.

Megan *halves the width of the sheet again.*

Megan   He drink so much he must a' been sick on 'em.

Megan *walks towards* **Bug** *and takes the sheet off him.*

Bug   He's dead.

Megan *halves the length of the sheet.*

Megan   It gonna kill him one day.

Megan *halves the length of the sheet again.*

Bug   Dint have no pain.

Megan *halves the length of the sheet again.*

Megan   Bet his liver do.

Megan *folds the sheet, folds it again and again.*

Bug   He talked about you –

Megan   Don't.

Beat.

Megan   Don't say no more.

Bug *leaves.* **Megan** *holds the tightly folded sheet to her chest as if it were the dead's flag.* **Mrs Peel** *enters, eyes* **Megan** *shaking from behind.*

Mrs Peel   You holdin' yourself again?

Megan *nods slowly.* **Mrs Peel** *shakes her head, sights the rest of the garments.*

Mrs Peel   Fold the rest a' the them things.

Megan *leaves with the sheet.*

Mrs Peel   You come back here.

Mrs Peel *storms after* **Megan** *but stops dead in her tracks as* **Burns** *enters, holding the radio.*

Mrs Peel (*Gruff.*)   What d'you want?

Mrs Peel *looks away from* **Burns***; he stays where he is.*

Mrs Peel   We goin' after my deer?

Mrs Peel *looks at* **Burns**.

Mrs Peel   Where's the supplies?

Mrs Peel *looks searchingly at* **Burns**.

Mrs Peel   Burns?

Burns *turns up the volume, beautiful music plays, and puts the radio down.*

Burns (*softly*)   I want my dance.

Mrs Peel (*Relieved but stern.*)   I aint dancin'.

Burns *walks towards* **Mrs Peel**.

Mrs Peel   Are you outta your mind! I aint dancin' in here! I got work to do! I never said when!

Burns *stands still before* **Mrs Peel**.

Burns   We only got now.

Burns *takes* **Mrs Peel**'s *hand. They dance; he is surprisingly light on his toes whilst she is as stiff as a fence post. He looks at her whilst she looks away. Gradually their steps become smaller and smaller until they are stood still.* **Burns** *looks at* **Mrs Peel** *for what feels like a long time but is only a moment, she looks back at him. They lean very slowly towards one another. They kiss.*

Turner (*Offstage.*)   Why'd you leave without me?

Bug (*Offstage.*)   Told you I was comin' back.

Mrs Peel *jolts away from* **Burns** *and darts over to the radio.* **Mrs Peel** *tunes the radio as* **Turner** *and* **Bug** *walk in.*

Turner   You could a' woke me up.

Bug   Thought you were stayin' on.

Turner   Well I thought both a' us were.

Mrs Peel   Quiet!

Radio (*American.*)   . . . resulting in the disarmament of the airbase and the withdrawal of the British Security from the Sheffield area which took place at ten hundred hours GMT. Plans today were revealed for a monument to commemorate the fallen dead in China.

Turner   Withdrawal?

Beat.

Turner   What's the disarmament of the airbase got to do with us?

Beat.

Turner   What the fuck does . . . withdrawal mean?

Burns   Means we aint there no more.

Turner   But . . . if we aint there then who is?

Beat.

Who's controllin' Sheffield?

Beat.

Turner   No, no, they . . . they bein' quarantined. S'why we pulled out. Fuck, I don't know, there enough diseases. (*To* **Mrs Peel**.) Put our radio on.

Burns   It's dead.

Turner   What d'you mean?

Turner *goes to the radio . . . it's dead.*

Turner   You gonna tell me what the fuck's going on?

Burns   I put it on this mornin' at around five and it was dead. I left for the station cause I had to pick up the supplies and the freight never showed. What? Why? Station aint even in Sheffield.

Burns   What did you hear in the beginnin'?

Mrs Peel   Ultimatum expired.

Turner   What ultimatum?

Mrs Peel   Dint hear no more

Turner   I'm . . . I'm . . . I don't know what's goin' on.

Burns   Civilians gave an ultimatum?

Turner   We gave one to them? We gave 'em an ultimatum, right?

Burns   We the ones who've withdrawn.

Turner   We don't know what that means.

Burns   Means we pulled –

Turner   I know that! We don't know why.

Mrs Peel   Why's it been broadcast over there?

Turner   Cause a' the airbase, it's theirs.

Mrs Peel   Why a' they here?

Turner   They're not anymore. Security gonna be headin' over there.

Burns   Maybe civilians a' headin' out there.

Turner   The Sheffield border'll still be there.

Burns   Said withdrew from the area. Area? Area? That aint specific.

Beat.

Burns   We ride out, see what's goin' on.

Mrs Peel   Aint it better to wait here?

Burns If they comin', no.

Turner They aint comin' out here, there gonna be Security from all over.

Burns (*To* **Mrs Peel**.) we'll go to a settlement, ask there.

Turner (*To* **Bug**.) You comin'?

Burns   You stay here till we get back.

Turner *leaves.* **Burns** *and* **Mrs Peel** *look at each other, at* **Bug** *stood in the distance between them, then back at each other.*

Burns   I'll be goin' then.

Burns *makes to leave.*

Mrs Peel   How long you gonna be?

Burns   Few hours.

They look at **Bug** *(oblivious that he is an obstacle) and then at the floor.*

Mrs Peel   How many?

Burns   Four.

Mrs Peel   Four?

Burns   Five, maybe.

They look at each other.

Burns   Can't say for sure.

Mrs Peel   No, course not.

Burns *makes to leave; stops.*

Burns   About yesterday . . .

Mrs Peel *looks at* **Bug**.

Mrs Peel   What about it?

Burns   The way I . . .

Burns *looks at* **Bug**.

Burns   Don't want yer to think that I just wanted . . .

They both look at **Bug**, *then at each other.*

Burns   I could sit and listen to you say the alphabet.

Beat.

Turner (*Offstage.*)   Burns!

Burns   I gotta go now.

Burns *leaves.* **Mrs Peel** *stands still for a few seconds; feels his absence. She starts folding the washing that* **Megan** *left behind. The rain continues to pour.*

Bug   You remember the drizzle, Mrs Peel?

Beat.

Bug   Constant . . . steady. Never seemed to end, did it? People complained about that. But it dint really affect us much. we were used to it. But now, it's different. Violent . . . unpredictable. I been out in the worst a' it. Laid there at night listenin' to it. Thinkin' to myself this can't go on . . . and it always did. But now . . . I think the atmosphere's finally broken apart.

Mrs Peel *has stopped folding.*

Bug   You understand what I mean?

Beat.

Mrs Peel   I was out walkin' one time just after a downpour a' rain. The kind we weren't used to back then. I'm walkin' close to a stream and further down on a rock I see a deer. Mindin' its own business, grazin' it was. When out a' nowhere, and at a deadly speed, a ragin' current a' water is comin' right at it. Deer freezes as the water rises all around it. Before, life was like a meanderin' stream. Takin' its time. Movin' casually. Now, it's like a flash flood. Deceptive. Can get you anytime.

Mrs Peel *picks up the pile of washing.*

Bug   What the deer do?

Mrs Peel   It got the fuck out a' there.

Mrs Peel *leaves.*

Bug   Too late.

Scene Six

Kitchen. Afternoon. Four hours have passed. Rain.

Megan *is sat peeling potatoes.* **Mrs Peel** *is tuning the American radio – various scraps of news, weather, music – she switches it off. She goes to the window, stares out for a while. She comes away from the window and sits at the table. Pause.*

Mrs Peel   Takin' too much skin off.

Mrs Peel *fiddles with the potato peelings.*

Mrs Peel   Look at that, waste a' tater. (*Suddenly alert.*) That horses?

Mrs Peel *rushes to the window.*

Mrs Peel   Wind . . . just hearing the wind.

Mrs Peel *comes away from the window.*

Mrs Peel   I need to get that bird in the oven, it's as old as me and it'll end up as tough if I don't have it in long enough. You muckin' out them stables after that. Mulch some a' the shit inta soil. Then yer can give me a hand gettin' them sheep inta the byres . . . winter's on its way in . . . gotta pluck that bird . . . I'll peel them taters.

Mrs Peel *goes to* **Megan**.

Mrs Peel   Give me the knife.

Megan   I know how to peel a' tater.

Mrs Peel   You abusin' that tater.

Megan *lobs the tater.*

Megan   That's abuse.

Beat.

Mrs Peel   Pick it up.

Megan   You pick it up.

Mrs Peel   I dint throw it.

Megan   You thrown away everythin' else.

Mrs Peel   Watch your mouth.

Megan   Say what I want.

Mrs Peel   Not to me you won't.

Megan   You don't want a' hear it.

Mrs Peel   Damn right I don't.

Megan   None a' you did, none a' you ever did, all this is cause a' you.

Mrs Peel   You have no right –

Megan   I have my right cause you had everythin' and left me nothin'.

Mrs Peel   We're all payin' for it.

Megan   You made your bed and you lyin' in it.

Mrs Peel   How dare you.

Megan   You been told / you been warned.

Mrs Peel   I marched! I protested!

Megan   You knew what would happen.

Mrs Peel   We dint know it would be like –

Megan (*Screams.*)   You let it get to this! You let the sea rise and flooded cities, burst river banks and destroyed our houses. You used up oil, made cars stop, forced us inta towns. You made us share rooms, put us in factories, fed us rations, let us get sick. You let my brother die a' TB, made my mum hang herself, sent James to war . . . for a pipe . . . and you killed him . . .

Mrs Peel (*Shouts.*)   That's enough!

Megan (*Cries hideously.*)   You killed him.

Mrs Peel   Enough.

Megan (*Wails.*)   I have a baby.

(*Silence.*)

Mrs Peel   You stupid. Stupid. Stupid girl!

Pause.

Mrs Peel   How far gone?

Megan   Five months.

Mrs Peel   You tell me this now?

Megan   Dint want to get rid a' it.

Mrs Peel   You can't keep the damn thing!

Megan   It my baby.

Mrs Peel   You don't have that choice.

Megan   Made my choice.

Mrs Peel   You took that rod out?

Megan   It a gift.

Mrs Peel   No. no. you'll pay a price for it.

Turner, *blood on his clothes, enters.*

Mrs Peel   Where's Burns?

Turner   Where's Bug?

Mrs Peel (*Quietly.*)   Where's Burns?

Turner   Need to tell Bug . . . there's too many a' 'em . . . they, they comin' from everywhere . . . runnin' right past us

like we aint even there . . . like we nothin' . . . like we aint
what they afraid a' . . . where's Bug? Cause Burns . . . Burns
is off his horse runnin' among 'em askin' . . . askin' why they
runnin' . . . bullet come out a' nowhere . . . where's Bug?
Need to tell him Burns's dead . . . that we gotta get out a'
here cause . . . we been left. We been left behind. A train
took all Security North this mornin' and no one thought to
come the fuck out here and fuckin' tell us! (*Rage.*) Where's
Bug?

Mrs Peel (*To* **Megan.**)   Wait outside.

Turner (*Rage.*)   They fuckin' left us out here to burn!

Turner *wheels round erratically.*

Mrs Peel (*To* **Megan.**)   Now.

Turner   Where's Bug?

Megan *leaves.*

Mrs Peel   He aint here.

Turner *is still frantic when suddenly he stands still, calm.*

Turner   I'm dyin' for some breakfast.

Beat.

Mrs Peel   I make it way past seven.

Turner *laughs a little.*

Turner   Yeah, guess it is.

Turner *walks away, stops, his back to* **Mrs Peel.**

Turner   They been firin' nuclear missiles from the airbase.
Ultimatum expired. We're gettin' one back.

Turner *walks away,* **Mrs Peel** *goes after him.*

Mrs Peel   What d'you mean?

Turner *turns to* **Mrs Peel.**

Turner   Boom.

Turner leaves. **Mrs Peel** *steps backwards and sits in the chair where* **Megan** *sat before. She sits very still for a few seconds, then picks up a potato and peels it.* **Megan** *enters; watches* **Mrs Peel** *attempting to peel the potato with trembling hands. Pause.*

Mrs Peel *continues to peel the potato.*

Megan   It a good sign?

Mrs Peel *continues to peel the potato.*

Megan   Mrs Peel?

Mrs Peel *continues to peel.*

Megan   They risen like Burns said?

Mrs Peel *stops peeling.*

Megan   That what it mean?

Mrs Peel *looks at* **Megan**. *Pause.*

Mrs Peel   Yeah. Yeah. It do.

Megan   What that mean for us?

Mrs Peel   We'll soon find out.

Mrs Peel *wanders away.*

Megan   Where you goin'?

Mrs Peel   Make us a tea.

Scene Seven

Peak. Late afternoon.

Bug *is sat, holding his flask.* **Turner** *is stood.*

Turner   We gotta get up North.

Turner *looks at* **Bug** *who stares out vacantly.*

Turner   We got a' head up the Pennine Way.

Beat.

Turner   You hear what I said?

Beat.

Turner (*Kicks the flask.*)   Answer me you useless piece a' shit!

Beat. **Turner** *stiffens.*

Turner   Get up.

Beat.

Turner   Get up now.

Beat.

Turner   Get up we're goin'.

Beat.

Turner   Up. (*Kicks* **Bug***'s foot.*) Now.

Turner *walks away, stops, back turned to* **Bug***.*

Turner   Get up!

Turner *puts his hands on his hips.*

Turner   On your feet soldier.

Bug   There are soldiers runnin' blind through smoke as another bomb slams down.

Turner (*Barks.*)   On your feet soldier.

Bug   Some are fallin', some are dragged down by the man behind.

Turner   On your fuckin' feet!

Bug   The earth buries 'em there and then together as the explosion ploughs the earth.

Turner (*Screams.*)   That's an order!

Bug   There are soldiers waitin' for order to retreat.

Turner (*Despair.*)   That's an order.

Bug   There are soldiers tryin' to sleep where they are cause the order never comes.

Turner (*Breaking.*)   I order you.

Bug   Explosions gun fire cries.

Turner (*Begging.*)   I order you under the authority of the Security to your feet.

Bug   Just have to stay where they are.

Turner *turns to* **Bug**.

Turner   I order you under the authority of this government to your feet.

Beat.

Bug   I no longer recognize this government.

Turner *leaves.*

Bug   There's a man. Young. Never seen him before. There are men runnin' fallin' cryin' all around him. He's on his knees. Can't take my eyes off a' him. The earth ploughs up around him. None a' it seems to matter. He's waitin' there on his knees. Then the sudden shock a' it. Couple a' instinctive jerkin' movements before bein' covered in earth.

Bug *kneels, slowly hangs his head, waits.*

Scene Eight

Plot of land. Late afternoon, the light is fading fast.

Mrs Peel *enters holding a bag of seeds,* **Megan** *is with her.*

Megan   Why a' we leavin'?

Mrs Peel   No need for us to be here no more, is there?

Megan *shakes her head.*

Megan Don't seem real.

Mrs Peel It'll sink in soon enough.

Mrs Peel *starts sowing seeds.*

Megan There been a time when you and me were out here workin', and you spotted a hare munchin' away at your salad leaves. You snuck up behind and grabbed hold a' it. I followed you inta the kitchen and you dropped a blow on its neck. Hare froze as straight as a fence post. You held it whilst I pulled back the skin, and you must a' been hungry cause you chopped it up right there and then on the board inta chunks. I couldn't stop lookin' at them chunks cause they were movin'. Jitterin', like they were cold or somethin'. You put them chunks inta the pan and they still jitterin'. You put the heat on 'em and I say to you: them chunks are still alive! You say: they dead they just don't know it yet.

Beat.

Megan I feel like I'm alive and I just don't know it yet.

Megan *turns to* **Mrs Peel**, *she looks away.*

Mrs Peel Let's sow these seeds before it gets dark.

Mrs Peel *kneels down and sows.*

Megan Why a' you sowin' seeds?

Mrs Peel For the future.

Megan But we aint gonna be here.

Megan Who gonna tend to it?

Mrs Peel This soil don't need us. Everythin' that happens upon it – failure a' crops, spreadin' a diseases, flood, drought – don't mean nothin' to it. Only the sun matters. Where there's light there will be life. S'long as the sunrises all will be.

Megan You should a' said that a long time ago.

Mrs Peel I like keepin' busy.

Beat. **Megan** *stops sowing, sits back.*

Megan   I'm gonna have a baby, Mrs Peel.

Mrs Peel   I know.

Megan   I'm not gonna know how to do things.

Mrs Peel   You'll be fine.

Megan   Most a' things I know you told me.

Mrs Peel   You gonna be good at it, Megan.

Megan *looks at* **Mrs Peel**.

Mrs Peel   (*Softly.*) You're gonna be good.

Megan   (*Beams.*) You never said that before.

Mrs Peel   No. I should a'.

Megan   A' we gonna leave together?

Mrs Peel   If you want.

Megan   We gonna stay together?

Beat.

Mrs Peel   If you want.

Megan   I do. Where we gonna go?

Beat.

Mrs Peel   I spent my childhood in Cumbria. Used to go out on the Lakes with my father on weekends. We'd be out there in all weathers too, hail comin' at us, thunder rollin' in, bitin' winds. We'd stop and eat sandwiches on a brow lookin' out at them moors, at valleys covered in droves a' heather, and fells . . . fells white with snow. If I think about the places I been, and I been my fair share, those white fells a' the loveliest thing I ever seen. I'd like to go there. I'd like to see snow on the fells again.

Megan   But there won't be any.

Mrs Peel   No. There won't.

Megan   But we could still go there.

Mrs Peel *nods. She moves behind* **Megan***.*

Megan (*Turns to* **Mrs Peel***.*)   When a' we gonna leave?

Mrs Peel   We' leavin' at sunrise.

Megan   Tomorrow?

Mrs Peel (*Smiles.*)   Tomorrow.

Megan *turns her beaming face round.*

Mrs Peel *raises the knife and slits* **Megan***'s throat.*

Mrs Peel *stands motionless for a long time.*

A long shear of light. A series of low concussions.

Mrs Peel *kneels, takes the blade and slits her throat.*

The sun sets. The sun rises.

A shoot grows out of the earth.

Blackout.

9 781408 131381